RAISING
OURSELVES
TO THE
BAR

RAISING
OURSELVES
TO THE
BAR

PRACTICAL ADVICE AND
ENCOURAGEMENT FOR
THE NEXT GENERATION OF
MISSIONARIES
AND THEIR PARENTS

BRAD WILCOX
RUSSELL WILCOX

DESERET
BOOK

SALT LAKE CITY, UTAH

To avoid embarrassing the wonderful missionaries who have permitted me to quote them, actual names of the sisters and elders have been changed or not otherwise provided.

Library of Congress Cataloging-in-Publication Data

Wilcox, Brad.
　Raising ourselves to the bar : practical advice and encouragement for the next generation of missionaries and their parents / Brad Wilcox, Russell Wilcox.
　　p. cm.
　Includes bibliographical references and index.
　ISBN-13: 978-1-59038-793-1 (pbk.)
　1. Missionaries.　I. Wilcox, Russell.　II. Title.
　BV2091.W55 2007
　266'.9332—dc22   2007017586

Printed in the United States of America
Sheridan Books, Chelsea, MI

10　9　8　7　6　5　4　3　2　1

To the missionaries of the
Chile Santiago East Mission
and

To President and Sister Lindon J. Robison
of the Spain Málaga Mission (2004–2007)

CONTENTS

PART FIVE: SKILLS

▲ ▲ ▲

FOREWORD

Much has been said in recent years about "raising the bar" for missionaries, and it is obvious that the increased attention on producing better-prepared, more worthy missionaries has had a positive effect. With the introduction of the inspired missionary guide *Preach My Gospel*, most missions in the Church are reporting an increase in productivity even though many are operating with a complement of fewer missionaries. In October general conference in 2002, Elder M. Russell Ballard of the Quorum of the Twelve said, "What we need now is the greatest generation of missionaries in the history of the Church."[1] In April conference of 2005, Elder Ballard also said, "What we are asking leaders in every unit to do is to counsel together with parents and pray to find at least *one more* young man, above those already committed, who can be called to serve. . . . [God] will bless all of us in our efforts to inspire and motivate more of our youth and couples to serve a full-time mission."[2] In an effort to help, my son Russell and I have produced "one more" book on missionary service.

We find ourselves in a rather unique position to produce this manuscript since we served simultaneously: Russell in Málaga, Spain, and I as mission president in Santiago, Chile, where I served with the rest of the family. Russell and I experienced firsthand the declining number of missionaries in both of those missions. Due to the smaller number of missionaries, we saw sectors close and many needs go unmet. There are perhaps several reasons why fewer missionaries are being called. For one, the demographics of the Church have changed, and LDS families typically are not as large as they once were. It is clear that the pool of prospective missionaries is smaller than it used to be. Nevertheless, we can't help but feel that there are more young people swimming around in that pool who could successfully serve if all of us (including the prospective missionaries) would do just a little bit more to help them qualify and prepare.

We know the rewards of serving missions. We have seen countless blessings and miracles in our own lives as well as in the lives of others. We can't even imagine life without the relationships, capabilities, perspectives, and testimonies that resulted from our missions. That is what we want for others—many, many others.

In each chapter we share our combined insights and experiences on themes selected from *Preach My Gospel.* Then I share what my wife and I tried to do to prepare Russell before his mission. Next, Russell shares his response. Finally, we have prepared keys for action—specific suggested tasks that can be completed for, with, and by young people as they prepare. We hope the ideas and experiences offered will provide positive affirmation for most, instruction for some, and motivation for all.

When Elder Jeffrey R. Holland of the Quorum of the Twelve was directing the work in Chile, he said on several occasions, "The bar is not an obstacle to get over, but a vision to reach for."

Gospel standards remain the same. Expectations for missionaries are clearly delineated in scriptures and in directions from our prophet leaders. The bar is set. It is now time for more of us to meet the standards and expectations by raising ourselves to the bar.

ACKNOWLEDGMENTS

We appreciate Chris Schoebinger at Deseret Book who approached us about writing this book and encouraged the idea of a father-son collaboration. We are also grateful to Richard Peterson, Shauna Gibby, and Laurie Cook, who all worked so skillfully to turn our manuscript into a published book.

My wife, Debi, always acts as our greatest supporter as well as our first editor. She can see past the coal and find the diamonds. We also appreciate Wendee, Whitney, and David Wilcox for their feedback and encouragement.

We are grateful for the input of Ray T. Wilcox in the beginning of this project. He passed away when we were about halfway through. We were sad to go back to the pages where we had written about this great man and put the sentences in past tense. However, we feel deep gratitude for the Savior, the temple, and our knowledge of the plan of salvation, which allowed Grandpa's passing, though difficult, to be a peaceful and spiritual next step. From Tahiti to Ethiopia and Utah to Georgia, he was always a dedicated missionary.

Val C. Wilcox and Leroy and Mary Lois Gunnell have also offered great experience and expertise as they edited the manuscript. Others who provided valuable assistance were Eliot and Susan Wilcox and Tara Oberg. We also acknowledge the love and support of

Trish Green, who became Russell's fiancée just one week after the final manuscript was submitted.

Thanks also to Roger and Moana Wilcox, Chris and Cheryl Wilcox, Rick and Kim McCloskey, Kay Davenport, Doug and Kristy Gunnell, John and Kim Bytheway, Kenneth and Kathy Cope, and Bob and Helen Wells. They, along with many other family members and friends, did much to allow us to be able to serve our missions.

It is a joy for me to serve as a member of the Mission Presidents' Advisory Committee. Many of the discussions in our meetings have prompted and shaped ideas in this book. Russell and I gratefully acknowledge the chair, Elder Wayne S. Peterson of the Seventy, and other members of the committee: Stephen B. Allen (Arizona Tempe), Robert P. Swensen (Brazil Curitiba), and Peter B. Rawlins of the Missionary Department; Robert L. Bauman (California Oakland), Edwin C. Biddulph (Philippines Bacolod), Wynn R. Dewsnup (Utah Ogden), Timothy S. Evans (Mexico Monterrey West), Michael J. Glauser (Georgia Atlanta), Kevin L. Ludlow (Washington Spokane), Steven J. Lund (Georgia Atlanta), Christopher B. Munday (England Birmingham), Russell T. Osguthorpe (South Dakota Rapid City), Phillip G. Pulsipher (Micronesia Guam), Scott G. Waldram (DR Congo Kinshasa), and Stephen R. Covey (Dublin Ireland).

In a similar way, we appreciate the mission presidents and their wives, along with the mission couples, who served in Chile. Their positive influence on the Wilcox family will never be forgotten.

Finally, we thank the missionaries and members in Málaga and in Santiago. Russell and I each learned much from their examples, devotion, friendship, and wisdom.

Introduction

▲ ▲ ▲

MISSIONS—HARD ON THE SHOES BUT GOOD FOR THE SOUL

No golf balls in the fruit bowl,
No skis against the shower stall,
No barbells blocking traffic
Along the narrow downstairs hall,
No music playing loudly
To shake our upstairs bedroom wall,
But just a changed young elder
Who has received his mission call.

That's how Grandma Wilcox describes the metamorphosis that takes place as a missionary prepares to serve. The story of each call is different and intensely personal. Some newly called elders and sisters gather with their families to open their special envelopes, while others seek to be alone. Some rush to the encyclopedia or computer to look up information about distant countries, while others are already very familiar with the places where they will serve. Some immediately feel a quiet and humbling confirmation of the correctness of the call. For others, that confirmation comes over time. In serving a mission, some follow the examples of parents, older siblings, and relatives. Others courageously set out on their own with little or no family support.

Missionaries come from many nations and speak many languages. A young sister in Utah worries about learning Japanese and serving in Tokyo. A young man in Japan worries about learning English and serving in Utah. Virtually all have been endowed in holy temples. They are all set apart. Some enter the MTC in England, others in Spain, Brazil, Provo, or elsewhere. It doesn't matter where they begin the journey, only that it has begun, for though this is a journey that is hard on the shoes, it is good for the soul.

Upon arriving in Santiago, Chile, one sister missionary became discouraged. She had always dreamed of a mission and prepared with diligence. Still, the realities of mission life combined with homesickness and the challenge of having to learn Spanish were almost more than she could bear. At one low point she cried to her mission president, "What on earth were they teaching us in the MTC? It would have been better preparation to hose us down from head to toe, put us in a freezer, and then swear at us all day long." Admittedly, since her arrival it had been raining and the streets were filled with water. It had also been unusually cold, and she had faced some rude rejections. Nevertheless, her president had to tell her that praying to be hit by a bus so she could go home was not the best option.

About a month later the same sister wrote the following in her weekly report to her president: "The good news is that I can honestly say I don't hate it here anymore. Even though I'm gaining weight because the members feed me so much and get offended if I don't eat it, I'm doing better. In fact, I think I would be disappointed now if a bus hit me."

What made the difference? Time helped, but there was something more. She wrote, "I fasted last Sunday with a list of concerns and questions I wanted answered. What I got instead was a feeling that everything is going to be okay, that I am going to be fine, and that I just need to be patient. Hearing that from a person is one thing (and you hear it from everyone), but hearing it from God is totally different. It is the difference between hearing it and feeling it, knowing it in your head and knowing it in your heart. I can smile now without having to force it."

Things were looking brighter, but this sister could not foresee how her feelings would continue to change over the course of her mission. A year and a half later she wrote, "I can't believe my mission is almost over. It has gone so quickly. It's not fair. I want more time. I can't stand the thought of leaving these people who have come to mean so much to me. In the mission I have had my trials, but they all seem like nothing compared to what I have learned. There are times I have studied something in the morning and then used it that very day to answer a question that came up. There are times when I have felt guided to the exact spot where I have been needed and my companion and I were able to make a difference. I've learned about the power of faith. How am I going to bear it when they take off my name tag and I have to live without being a full-time missionary?"

Hers was a metamorphosis. And the same story can be told over and over as missionaries step up to the challenge and succeed. One elder wrote shortly after arriving in his mission: "I have lots of blisters on my feet, but don't worry, President. I don't really notice them because it is so cold." Later he wrote, "It's kind of frustrating when you can't understand the language. I want to work hard, but I can't communicate. All I can do is follow my comp around. But don't worry. I will never give up. If the Lord wants me to just nod and smile for two years, I will." Of course, this missionary learned the language and did a lot more than nod and smile. When it came time for his mission to end, he didn't want to leave either.

As another sister's mission drew to a close she wrote, "My mission has been the best time of my life. I've never felt so alone, been so frustrated, had so many pillows wet with tears and felt so for-saken, rejected, and insecure, but I can still say it has been the best time because I've never before been so close to my Savior. This work has become my passion. I knew I would love the work and the people, but this much? This is God's work and glory, but it has become my work and glory too. . . . I'm thankful for that night in the garden and that day on the cross—all that I might feel the joy I'm feeling now."

Russell's last e-mail from the mission said, "Is it normal to be afraid? Each day as the end gets closer I don't want to finish. I don't want to stop being a full-time missionary. I don't want to go home. . . . I am afraid to leave the people I love. I'm afraid I'm going to miss everything too much. I thought I would be excited to go home, but it's a lot more difficult than I imagined it would be. . . . I feel satis-fied and happy, very happy with my mission. I don't have regrets. I just don't like to think of this experience coming to an end."

Russell served in beautiful southern Spain. He would send his family pictures of the ocean and beautiful palm trees and green countryside. I served in the large and crowded city of Santiago. And I sent Russell pictures of skyscrapers, graffiti, litter, buses, and smog. Still, the outward conditions made no difference in how we felt about our missions. We know missionaries who have served in the coldest spots on earth and right in the middle of the driest deserts. It doesn't matter to them. Most finished their missions feeling just the same joy and satisfaction as Russell and I did. Some missionar-ies come home after an unhappy experience, but they are more the exception than the rule.

Missions include more than hard times. There is a lot of humor found along the way. Here are a few examples:

One missionary was transferred from a big city to a small, rural town. He said to his new comp, "At least now I am away from all the stray dogs." Little did he know that as they rode their bikes that afternoon they would be attacked by pigs that chased them down the street. He said, "Great! The dogs have been replaced with killer pigs!"

A new elder was working hard to memorize the baptismal prayer. That explains why he shocked the member providing him lunch when he closed his blessing on the food "in the name of the Father, and of the Son, and of the Holy Ghost. Amen."

One new sister missionary almost blew up her house because she had never used a gas stove before. When all the neighbors came rushing to help, she and her companion ended up giving out three copies of the Book of Mormon and setting two teaching appointments. She told her mission president, "Maybe we ought to try the same approach in other parts of the mission!"

When New Year's Day fell on a Sunday a missionary wrote, "We had only 31 members show up at church and later we counted 35 drunks plastered in the park. Hmmm. It looks like Satan is ahead by four!"

Two elders showed up at the home of a member who graciously was providing them lunch. When she filled their plates, the older missionary recognized the dish as cow's stomach and lost his appetite. Not knowing what he was eating, the younger missionary dove right in. The older missionary then asked his companion to eat his helping as well so as to not offend the cook. Just as they were trading plates, the woman entered the room. She said, "Oh, elder! I'm sorry you don't like your lunch. I will fix you something different." She disappeared into the kitchen and returned with a plate of salmon. The Elder didn't have the heart to tell her he was deathly allergic and so he waited till she was gone and piled the salmon on his companion's plate as well. When the missionaries left, one was so full he could hardly walk and the other was starving!

Another funny experience happened when a new sister who didn't speak Spanish very well was listening to a man talk about his suicide attempt, and all the while she thought he was talking about his baptism (complete with tears). You can imagine his face when she said happily, "How wonderful that you had such a good experience!"

With a good dose of both struggles and joy, hardships and humor, missions change us forever. Missions change others as well. One young boy and his brother heard their parents fighting again in the kitchen. When they heard their father hit their mom they rushed in to try to defend her. She worried that they would also get hurt and so she pushed them out the door and locked them outside. These little boys didn't know what they could do to help their mom so they prayed to God. As they finished, two young men with white shirts came walking down the street. The boys rushed up to them and told them what was happening in their home. The two missionaries hurried to the house and courageously knocked on the door. That was the beginning of big changes for the family. Now both those boys are grown up and serving their own missions.

A convert from Argentina first became interested in the Church when a friend at school kept giving him the coffee-flavored candy he didn't want. When asked why, the friend said, "I'm a Mormon and we don't drink coffee so I don't like that flavor." That simple explanation opened the door to this young man attending Church, meeting with missionaries, getting baptized, and later serving a mission.

Two missionaries made a contact with a couple in the street. After visiting for a minute, one of the elders said, "Have you ever met Mormon missionaries before?" The man said, "The truth is that I *was* one about ten years ago." It turns out he was an inactive returned missionary who had married outside the Church. His wife didn't even know he had been a missionary. As they began attending church together, he became active again and eventually she was baptized.

A pair of elders was walking down the street and greeted a woman they passed. Several blocks later the one looked at the other and said, "Are you feeling what I am feeling?" The other said, "Yes. We were supposed to talk to that woman." They ran back to talk to her. She ended up giving them an address, but it turned out to be one she just made up to get rid of them. The elders weren't too upset—especially when the people who lived at the fictitious address ended up joining the Church.

These are just a few examples of the impact missionaries have worldwide. Most people can't name winners of the Nobel Prize without looking them up. They can't name the people who make the largest charitable donations or win the most gold medals or Academy Awards. Perhaps some people know such answers, but we don't. However, we can tell of missionaries who made a difference in our lives. Some were from early Church history. Some have served with us. In one way or another, directly or indirectly, every member of the Church has felt the influence of missionaries, and we are all better for it.

Part One:

PURPOSE

▲ ▲ ▲

"Your purpose [is to] invite others to come unto Christ
by helping them receive the restored Gospel. . . .
As an authorized representative of Jesus Christ,
you can teach people with power and authority."

Preach My Gospel, *1–2*

1

▲ ▲ ▲

GOD: HE LOVES ME—
SATAN: HE LOVES ME NOT

"Why did Satan tempt Adam and Eve?" asked a missionary. Initially the elder thought the temptation was an effort to destroy God's plan, but upon more careful study, he realized that Satan's actions actually moved the plan along. "So, why would he want to help God?" the elder then asked.

The missionary needed to learn that God loves us and Satan loves us not. Satan has absolutely no intention of giving God a hand. Moses tells us that Satan "knew not the mind of God" (Moses 4:6), but Satan did know the plan of salvation. He was there in the premortal existence and had no veil placed over his memory. He also knew Adam and Eve. So the only reason Satan would tempt them was if somehow their behavior benefited him—and it did.

Satan wanted to get the show on the road because the sooner Adam and Eve had children, the sooner the adversary could do damage. Until there were souls to steal, Satan's work was at a standstill. He knew he had no chance of winning, so in his complete and total wickedness, his only desire was to deceive and pull away as many of God's children as he could, "for he seeketh that all men might be miserable like unto himself" (2 Nephi 2:27), whereas God's work and glory is "to bring to pass the immortality and eternal life of man" (Moses 1:39). Satan's work is to thwart that plan by keeping as many as he can from being able to live with God and loved ones eternally. To the extent that he succeeds in that evil scheme, Satan hurts Heavenly Father and Jesus to the core.

Satan claims to reign as "prince of this world" (John 12:31) with no one to frighten him. That's where he is wrong. He is overlooking all of us. We may not look like much, but Satan has reason to fear because we have authority that he will never have.

Satan's power is external and dependent. It is put on—like an apron. Had he no followers, his authority would disappear. Christ's power, on the other hand, is internal and independent. As true messengers of Christ, missionaries are endowed with his authority.

A new missionary arrived in Chile and was struggling with the language, culture, and feelings of homesickness. Nevertheless, he knew who he was. In the middle of a missionary lesson the elders were teaching, a man pulled out a cigarette and lit it. The senior companion asked if he would mind waiting to smoke until after the lesson, but the man continued to smoke. The senior companion said it was disturbing them and would he please wait until after they left. The man went right on smoking. That's when the newly arrived elder spoke up and in his broken Spanish said, "We are representatives of the Lord Jesus Christ. Smoking in our faces is like smoking in His face." The man put out the cigarette for the rest of the lesson. The new missionary was not rude and did not even raise his voice. Boldness doesn't require a raised voice. The elder simply spoke the truth.

In 3 Nephi 28:34 we read: "And wo be unto him that will not hearken unto the words of Jesus, and also to them whom he hath chosen and sent among them; for whoso receiveth not the words of Jesus and the words of those whom he hath sent receiveth not him; and therefore he will not receive them at the last day."

Another missionary and his companion were walking through a busy park when a man called to them. The man's brother had died, and he was looking for some answers. He wanted to draw closer to God. The missionaries were able to set up a time to visit him at his home. The missionary later wrote, "Of all the people there and all the people he could have turned to in his sorrow, he turned to a couple of kids. Why? Because something told him we were more than a couple of kids. We are representatives of the Lord Jesus Christ and he recognized that. It was a humbling experience."

A sister missionary wrote, "On Friday we stopped by the house of a new convert whose husband is not a member. He went on and on about how stupid the people were in Christ's day because they didn't recognize him and listen to him when he was right in front of them. How ironic. There we were—two representatives of Jesus Christ—right in front of him and he didn't recognize us or listen to us. History just repeated itself."

An elder wrote, "I bore my testimony to a woman about the Book of Mormon, and as I did she felt something. She told us, 'You know, as you spoke to me just now I felt as if Jesus were speaking, as if he were here and I were listening to him teach on the mount. I know that's impossible, but that is what I felt.'"

Two elders were knocking on doors on a street and as they were talking to one lady, a little girl several doors down ran to get her mother. She kept saying, "It is Jesus. Mom, Jesus is coming to our house." The mother saw the elders and told the girl, "No, that's not Jesus. It's just the Mormons." The girl persisted in saying, "No, Mom, it is Jesus. I know it."

In Spain, Russell and his companion were teaching a woman who was deaf. The missionaries did not know sign language, but she was able to read their lips, and occasionally her son was there to translate. Russell remembers teaching her about how through the atonement of Jesus Christ we would all be resurrected in perfect form. He had taught the concept many times to mixed reactions, but never had he seen someone respond as she did. Through her son she asked if that meant she would be able to hear. When the elders said yes, she closed her eyes and smiled as if imagining how it would be. Her face was filled with a sweet look of comfort and anticipation. The elders continued teaching that through the Atonement we can repent of our sins and be succored in our afflictions—that Jesus knows what we are going through. Here was a woman who knew afflictions and desired the succoring of which the missionaries spoke. Of all those with ears to hear, it was a deaf woman who really listened. At the end of their visit, Russell asked her to teach him the sign for *missionary*. She touched the middle finger of her left hand to the center of the palm of her right and then repeated the action from right to left—nail marks. Russell asked, "Isn't that the sign for Jesus?"

Her son translated her response: "It's the same thing. In Spanish sign language, Jesus and missionary are the same sign."

Wherever there are true messengers, Satan cowers and ultimately retreats. His lack of authority is exposed. His position is threatened, and that makes him angry. Does he throw a tantrum when somebody gives money to charity, helps a neighbor, or when another church builds a building? It can't please him, but it doesn't make him truly mad. Many good people do many positive things, but it doesn't frighten Satan or set him back because he knows that no matter how good these things might be, they are only temporary. However, principles, practices, and ordinances in the true Church are different for they have the potential to change eternity—and not just for one person but also for that person's ancestors and posterity. That messes Satan up in a big way. That is a blow from which he can't recover. That's why he fights against us with such venomous hatred.

In the middle of the city of Santiago is a hill called Cerro San Cristobal. It would be a wonderful place from which to see the view, except that the smog in Santiago is usually so thick no one can see much. Still, it was fun to ride the little tram to the top, and I would sometimes go there with new missionaries.

One day we were with an elder who was a convert to the Church before his mission. He had already been influential in helping other members of his family join. As he rode the tram to the top of the hill, this Chilean missionary noticed a plaque commemorating the visit of the Pope to Santiago and identifying that very car as the one in which he rode to the top of the hill. This elder was impressed and kept saying, "I can't believe I am standing in the exact spot where the Pope stood." I said, "Elder, I am sure the Pope is a good man and deserves our respect, but I am going to have another plaque made that says: *Elder Garcia rode in this very car and he has more priesthood authority than any pope, king, or president in the world.*" Elder Garcia considered these words and then the truth hit him. We sometimes describe such a moment as "when the light turned on." In actuality, it is more accurate to talk about when the light came *in*. The Spirit touched Elder Garcia's spirit, and he understood. There is no doubt that in the world's view of things, popes and other world leaders have more authority, but in reality Elder Garcia had more potential to affect Santiago in the long run. God knew it and now Elder Garcia knew it, and that threatens Satan's work.

In that week's letter to the mission president, Elder Garcia wrote, "It's fun to make Satan furious. I can't think of anything I would rather do. I love my job!" Similarly, a sister missionary once posted a note on her mirror that said, "Live so that every morning Satan says, 'Oh, no! She's up!'"

Just as we can make Satan mad, we also can make Heavenly Father and Jesus happy—not just temporarily, but eternally. We can bring them joy and glory that lasts. Upon realizing this, one missionary said in his testimony, "Jesus and God have cried enough tears. I want to give them a smile for a change."

That's exactly what we can do. We have authority. We have

complete truth. Now we must match that authority with power and that truth with dedicated discipleship. *Who* we are, by virtue of our lineage, birth, and blessings, is not nearly as important as *whose* we are, by virtue of our baptism and faithfulness. The lineage in our blood is not nearly as important as His image in our countenances. Having been saved for the last days means little if we are not saving others.

We hear often that we are children of God and that he loves us, but such a testimony is incomplete if we, like some of the children of Adam and Eve, choose to love "Satan more than God" (Moses 5:13). Young women in the Church know that it is not enough to declare only that they are daughters of a Heavenly Father who loves them. They must add, "and we love him. We will stand as witnesses of God at all times, and in all things, and in all places."

Satan, the so-called prince of this world, is reigning with blood and terror. As his time gets shorter, he is turning up the heat, and he thinks there is no one to stand in his way. He'd better think again! We are not going to lie down and let him reign unopposed. We are not letting him pursue his evil purposes without a fight. We, as did Jesus, will stand up to him and say, "Get thee hence" (Matthew 4:10).

When the world was created, the Lord said, "Let there be light; and there was light . . . and [he] called the light Day; and the darkness . . . Night" (Moses 2:3–5). And he "made two great lights; the greater light to rule the day, and the lesser light to rule the night, and the greater light was the sun, and the lesser light was the moon" (Moses 2:16). From the beginning the world has never been left in complete darkness. Even at night, light always rules.

During the Great Apostasy—a time very appropriately called the Dark Ages—there was still light. The priesthood was not generally available to man, but there was still priesthood on the earth. Because of the promises made to John the Beloved and the Three Nephites, the world was never totally abandoned to darkness.

Satan knew the Restoration would bring a flood of light and priesthood keys. He did everything he could to keep that from happening. Right up until seconds before the First Vision, Satan was giving it all he had to try to bind Joseph Smith. But as that darkness threatened to destroy Joseph, "at the very moment when [he] was ready to sink into despair and abandon [himself] to destruction," he saw "a pillar of light. . . . It no sooner appeared," said Joseph, "than I found myself delivered from the enemy which held me bound" (Joseph Smith—History 1:16–17). Satan hates light because when light and darkness meet, darkness always loses.

Satan knows that every mission represents a "restoration" of sorts in someone's life. As a consequence of faithful missionary service, someone, somewhere, is going to be lifted out of his or her own "dark ages" into the light. That is why Satan tries so hard to stop us from serving missions, just as he tried to stop Joseph from receiving the vision that marked the beginning of this work. Each missionary is as important in bringing light into someone's world as Joseph was in bringing light to the whole world.

As dark as it sometimes seems and as discouraged as we sometimes become, light always rules. The only power Satan has is what we choose to give him. God will never leave us alone. God loves us and Satan loves us not. "That which is of God is light; and he that receiveth light, and continueth in God, receiveth more light; and that light groweth brighter and brighter until the perfect day" (D&C 50:24).

WHAT I TRIED

One of the hardest things for parents to do is to try to help their children see beyond the image facing them in the mirror each morning. Sometimes I wish the veil were not drawn quite so tightly over their memories, so our children could more easily see themselves the way God sees them.

That perspective is sometimes hard to find and maintain amid the mood swings, broken curfews, and insecurities of adolescence. Some days our teenage children hate us. Some days they hate themselves. Often they reject love and attention when it is needed the most.

Like most parents, my wife and I have tried to stay positive and upbeat while working to rear our children. When Russell was growing up, we always told him that he could be anything he could envision, even though he seemed to change his mind about what he wanted to be every other week! With Russell, as with all our children, Debi and I have tried to notice and encourage the good things they are doing and planning. We have tried to spend time together as a family, so the children would know they are a priority. Like most parents, we *know* what we should do. The challenge is in *doing it*—even when we ourselves are feeling pressured, worn out, and underappreciated.

For me it is quite easy to see the eternal goodness and great potential of my children. It just shines—even on difficult days. It is much harder for me to see it in myself. When it comes to parenting, I am painfully aware of my own weaknesses. For me it is easy to encourage my children by saying, "You can do it." But when I turn those same words on myself, I sometimes struggle to believe them.

It is on those days when I am feeling very mediocre that I have to remember that the word *mediocre* comes from the Latin word, *mediocris,* which means "halfway up the mountain." No one stands on top of a mountain without passing through the halfway point. That doesn't mean the halfway point is as far as I can go. It only means that is as far as I have come. Perfection is my ultimate goal in parenting and in everything else, but I have to remember that perfection is not something that has to be accomplished by next Saturday. Mediocrity is a stage through which we all must pass on our way to greatness. I'm headed to the top of the mountain, but it is going to take me a little time to get there. I have to be patient with myself and learn to see my efforts—however feeble—as worthwhile.

RUSSELL'S RESPONSE

Dad is right about my changing my mind a lot. As a child I wanted to do just about everything. I wanted to be a professional basketball player one day and a taxi driver in New York City the next. Not once did my parents ever trample my dreams, question my talents, or tell me I couldn't do something. My childhood memories are of constant encouragement and support from parents and also from teachers, relatives, and Church leaders. I remember my dad taking me to a big magic show on my birthday and spending the whole time building me up, complimenting me, and focusing on my positive traits. Believe me, with all that attention, I was one happy kid.

As a teen, I began to struggle more with my self-image. I became preoccupied with who was "in" and who was "out" at school. Suddenly, who my friends were and what sports I played or didn't play became very important to me. I worried much more about what my peers thought about me than what my parents thought about me. (Sorry, Mom and Dad, but it's true.) Being accepted by peers became all-important, and I even found myself doing things I knew I shouldn't in an effort to gain that acceptance.

Luckily, I got a job at a jewelry store near my home where I worked with college students. We became great friends, and they taught me big "college" words. We talked about dating, and they showed me how to match my tie with my pants (something I had not thought was all that important up till then). They lifted my eyes away from the peer group that surrounded me at school and helped me see a bigger world. They taught me that it didn't matter quite so much who I hung out with or if I made the team. I liked and respected these people, and I never thought once about how popular they were in high school, who they hung out with, or what sports they played. I liked them because they were good people, not because they could make me more popular.

Missionaries can do for others what my friends in the jewelry store did for me. They can lift the eyes of their investigators away from the peer group that surrounds them and help them see a broader perspective. They can help them realize how much the Savior loves them.

KEYS FOR ACTION

What Can We Do FOR Young People?

One father said, "When my children became teenagers, I realized quickly that I needed to have eyes in the back of my head. Now I guess I need to train those eyes to see the positive and ignore the negative." Most of us tend to notice the weed instead of the garden, the graffiti instead of the building, and the one C instead of the five A's on the report card. Is it surprising that young people feel inadequate when their adequacy is rarely noticed by adults in their lives?

A teenage girl was mowing the lawn and the lawnmower broke down. She asked her dad what she should do, and he suggested she borrow the neighbor's mower to finish up. Within a few minutes the girl interrupted her father yet again, asking if he knew how to start the neighbor's mower. With a sigh, the dad left his work and went outside to start the mower. As he began to demonstrate, the daughter gave him an exasperated look that said she was in no mood for explanations. That's when the dad's patience gave way, and he snapped at her. Then he felt terrible. Instead of recognizing his daughter for mowing the lawn without even being asked and for not giving up even when the mower broke, he got upset at her. To his credit, he quickly apologized.

Praise nourishes the spirit just as food nourishes the body. We know how much food a growing teenager's body can take in. How much food are we offering their growing spirits? When was the last time we wrote a little note of praise and left it on a child's pillow? When was the last time we praised children for getting up and ready for seminary or school? We wouldn't dream of sending a child off in the morning without clothes; yet how often do we send them off without the "garment of praise" for their spirit (Isaiah 61:3)?

Some people believe that giving liberal amounts of praise will make a child arrogant and conceited. I believe otherwise—that praising a child builds confidence and security. I believe it helps children define and internalize who they are. There are enough self-appointed critics around to point out faults, emphasize problems, and list reasons why young people can't achieve their dreams. Parents need to counter such voices. We need to be the ones cheering young people on, offering hope, noticing the good, celebrating the victories, and treating them with respect. In doing so we are only following the example of Heavenly Father, who said of Jesus, "This is my beloved Son, in whom I am well pleased" (Matthew 3:17).

What Can We Do WITH Young People?

There is no better way to internalize who we are than to prepare for and receive our patriarchal blessings. Such blessings can be a great help to both children and parents. One young man— handsome, athletic, and popular—seemed to have everything going for him. However, his dad knew of weaknesses others didn't see in his outwardly admirable son. He saw, for instance, the outrageous cell-phone bills the young man was racking up because he simply would not stop calling and text-messaging girls he would meet around the state at athletic events.

The boy surprised his father one day by asking about patriarchal blessings. There had been a lesson on the topic given in seminary, and this young man had determined it was time to get his blessing. His dad helped him set up an appointment with the bishop, who signs the form recommending a person to the patriarch. When the day of the blessing arrived, the father was astonished to hear the incredible promises being made to his son. Was this the same immature kid who was costing him a fortune in phone bills? When they arrived home, the father said, "Things are going to change around here. We're going to start having family prayer and family home evening again. We're going to start our family scripture study again, too. I'm going to do all I can to make this home a better training camp for you."

During the following year, whenever the father was frustrated by his son's immature behavior, he would recall the blessing and focus on his son's great potential. Similarly, whenever the son became tempted or discouraged, he would read his blessing and feel inspired to do better.

What Can Young People Do BY THEMSELVES?

Russell mentioned the power and influence of the college-aged friends at work who became positive role models for him. Just as Russell did, all young people can find heroes. Of course, the Savior is the ultimate hero for us all. It is also important to look for heroes in the scriptures or among the general authorities, but most of us don't hang out with Captain Moroni or have the prophet come to dinner. Along with heroes admired from afar, we need heroes close at hand—*touchable* heroes.

Elder Vaughn J. Featherstone of the First Quorum of the Seventy once wrote about an encounter with a stake president who had a profoundly positive effect on him. Elder Featherstone said, "As I left his home that night, I wanted to be the kind of gentleman he was. I wanted to live the way he lived. . . . I had experienced one of those 'images of greatness' that would help set a pattern for the kind of man I wanted to be."[3]

Adults can create opportunities for young people to meet such images of greatness—at camps, youth conferences, firesides, Especially for Youth gatherings, etc., but it is really up to young people themselves to select, from among their acquaintances and those they meet, worthy heroes they can look at and say, "If they can do it, I can do it."

2

▲ ▲ ▲

GOD PARTED THE RED SEA, AND HE WILL HELP YOU THROUGH YOUR MISSION, TOO

"What's wrong?" asked Russell of one of the missionaries he was teaching in the MTC. For days he had noticed the elder was unfocused, unenthused, and far from being "anxiously engaged." Russell pulled him aside to talk with him one-on-one.

"I don't know," the elder replied. "I just don't think I can do this. It's not what I expected and I'm not enjoying it. How am I going to last two years? I think I just want to go home."

Russell's thoughts unfolded like a test question: What does this missionary need? A) a firm lecture on his responsibility, B) a scripture or quote about the importance of missionary work, C) a warning about what would happen if he went home, D) all of the above, or E) none of the above. Russell chose the final option. How could he give him a lecture or warning when only a couple of years earlier he had been in the same MTC feeling the same way? Instead of lecturing, Russell said, "Hey, does it help to know you're not alone? I can't tell you how many times I wrote *two years seems like forever* in my journal when I first started."

"Really?" asked the young missionary. He had never imagined his teacher would have felt that way (or at least would admit it so openly).

Russell told him, "I think most missionaries feel that way at first. Everyone has thoughts about going home, but I'm glad I didn't and you will be, too."

We sing in a favorite missionary hymn, "I'll go where you want me to go, dear Lord"[4] but maybe we need to add a few words: "I'll go where you want me to go, dear Lord—and stay there." No one in the Church is ever forced to do anything. No one is forced to go on a mission any more than we are forced to receive our endowments. In the temple we are all given the opportunity to leave if we do not want to make commitments. No one has to stay, but once we choose to stay, integrity demands that we lock the door on any escape hatch, turn our faces forward, smile, and stick with it to the end.

Elder David S. Baxter of the First Quorum of the Seventy said, "The Savior's parable of the wise man who built his house upon a rock has power precisely because it illustrates that life's challenges befell the wise man, too. The rains fell, the winds blew, the floods rose up. Yet he survived it all because he had built upon a sure foundation and, crucially, he stayed there when the storm came."[5]

God didn't remove the Red Sea, but he provided a way for the children of Israel to go through it. In the same way, God doesn't remove the requirement of mission service or the difficulty of meeting that challenge. Instead, he helps us through it. There are lots of reasons we go on missions (some of them noble and some not so noble). No matter what gets us out there, God will provide what we need to make it through. For Russell and me it had a lot to do with living, laughing, loving, lifting, and learning.

LIVING

Missions are made up of extremes. We are rarely just happy or sad. We are usually extremely happy or extremely sad, but that's okay.

When we get hooked up to the heart monitor, we definitely don't want to see a straight line. The ups and downs are a healthy indicator. It means we are alive—participating and not observing, paddling and not coasting.

An elder from Spain said, "From day one I wondered if I would be able to make it through. I remember my first day in the MTC, looking out the window and thinking, *What have I done?* But now I think of the people who have helped me. I think of the miracles I have seen. We have placed our hands on people and seen them healed. I have had meaningful dreams and personal revelation. I have seen people baptized. I have never fasted and prayed for people so much."

In Ezekiel is a beautiful prophecy that speaks of waters coming from the house of the Lord, offering life and healing to all they touch: "And every thing shall live whither the river cometh" (Ezekiel 47:9). Although this prophecy has to do with the temple and the Savior, it also has a lot to do with missions.

Before their missions, most young people derive their self-esteem from everything from high school athletics or activities to college scholarships. They see their worth in terms of popularity or grades. They have defined themselves based on their jobs, cars, music, and number of text messages they receive from friends.

Suddenly they find themselves on a mission, where such things don't matter very much. Members and investigators care little about what awards they won before they came out or how much money they earned. They care only about whether the missionary cares about them and is doing the work of the Lord.

It is likely that until the young missionary catches on, he or she will feel as though everything that mattered in life has been stripped away. All that was familiar and comfortable gets left behind until the only thing that remains is God. And suddenly the missionary starts building his self-esteem on the relationship he has with God, which is where it should have built in the first place. The river spoken of in Ezekiel touches him and he lives. Finally he understands what the Savior was teaching when he said, "For whosoever will save his life shall lose it; but whosoever shall lose his life for my sake and the gospel's, the same shall save it" (Mark 8:35). Of course, sports, friends, family, awards, jobs, and music will all fit back in when missions are over, but they will, I hope, never again be the foundation.

One sister missionary put it this way: "You can't believe in yourself without believing in God. You can't find yourself without finding him. You can't be yourself without being like him."

LAUGHING

President John Taylor said, "We like enjoyment here. That is right. God designs that we should enjoy ourselves. I do not believe in a religion that makes people gloomy, melancholy, miserable and ascetic."[6]

Similarly, President David O. McKay said, "We don't need to be long-faced and pious to be religious. We shouldn't be gloomy when we worship God; we should be happy. Sometimes I'm overwhelmed by the joy to be found everywhere."[7]

Learning a foreign language sometimes provides a lot of laughs. One elder stood in church to pray, but instead of blessing the ward he blessed the mud. Another got up and was trying to say he liked the Spanish language and instead announced he liked French-kissing. One sister asked a woman she met on the bus where she lived. The woman responded, "On the street Luis Mate." The new sister missionary thought the woman had said her name and ended up calling her Luis for weeks after.

While interviewing missionaries one time, I listened to one of the sister missionaries express her discouragement. Tearfully, she asked me if I thought she were *fea,* which means ugly. I misunderstood her and thought she had said *fiel,* which means faithful. You can image the sister's surprise when her mission president answered, "Yes, very!"

Two sister missionaries took some food to a member in need, but no one was home. They saw the little kitchen window was open and decided to slide the container through the window. However, when they dropped the container it accidentally turned the water on in the sink and simultaneously blocked the drain. The sink began to fill, and they knew it would soon flood the house. Heaven only knows what the neighbors thought when they saw two Mormon missionaries breaking into the house next door.

Two other sisters dropped their clothes off at the home of a sister in the ward who had volunteered to do their laundry. When no one answered their knock, they left the clothes on the front porch with a note that said, "Thanks for doing our wash. We will be back about 1:00 for lunch. Love, the sister missionaries." They didn't realize it was the wrong house! When the lady of the house returned and read the note she was confused but went ahead and washed the clothes and prepared lunch anyway. It turns out she was an inactive member who took the whole thing as a sign that she needed to come back to church.

Elder Neal A. Maxwell wrote, "There is a special gladness that goes with the gospel, and appropriate merriment."[8] He also wrote, "Zion . . . is where the pure in heart dwell and where there is joy of countenance. By contrast, in hell there are no smiles!"[9]

It has been our experience that part of the joy to be found in serving missions comes from having appropriate fun and discovering the funny things that unexpectedly happen as a regular part of missionary service.

LOVING

One missionary said, "At the beginning of my mission I asked my mom to send packages filled with things for me. Now I ask for packages filled with stuff I can give away."

Another missionary experienced the same growth. He said, "My mission has changed me a lot. I actually care about the spiritual well-being of other people. Not many twenty-year-old boys care about that."

Our friend Barbara Barrington Jones calls it switching from channel one to channel two. If you are watching TV and you change channels, it doesn't mean that the original channel ceases to exist. It simply means you are no longer focused on it. The push of a button can easily bring it again to the forefront. In the same way, if we are to be successful and effective missionaries, we need to change channels in our lives and take the focus off *our* needs, *our* problems, and *our* worries (channel one) and put it on the needs of others (channel two).

Upon receiving a transfer, one elder wrote, "I am sad to leave the sector that has been the turning point of my mission. I had a convert crying last night—a teenager I've only known for a month, but it was so touching that his mother turned her head away, fighting tears. I had to turn away too. It was hard to say good-bye to such a beloved friend. In another house a young couple planned a small party with a little cake for the two elders who had introduced them to a new way of life and a deeper love for each other than they had known. After a lot of laughs, the time came for farewells. The husband asked me to say the prayer, and I just pled with Heavenly Father for the well-being and spiritual protection of this family that has come to mean so much to me. The prayer was a result of pure love. There is no greater work than this. It wasn't easy to leave the sector, but I did it with a feeling of contentment and fulfillment I have never known before in my life. Truly, my life will never be the same. I have learned to love."

Such love is the source of the sweetest moments of our lives, but it can also open the door to great pain. When you love you can easily get hurt and taken advantage of. Mother Teresa said, "Love anyway." A missionary wrote, "I sometimes feel I'm doing something wrong. But then I step back and realize I'm not doing anything wrong. There are just certain things I can't change. . . . I know every missionary feels frustrated, but this week I felt it to the point of crying. Why don't they listen? The truth of this message is so obvious. . . . Before, it hurt because I wanted baptisms. Now it hurts because they are good-hearted people, sons and daughters of God—brothers and sisters who are lost. That is what is starting to hit me. I used to hurt for me. Now I hurt for a new reason—love."

Such awareness is one of the sweetest benefits of missionary service. Ask anyone who has served a successful mission, and he will always talk about the people he met and the deep feelings of affection the missionary has for those he or she had the privilege of teaching—to say nothing of the love those people have for "their" missionary.

LIFTING

Missions give us a wonderful opportunity to lift others, sometimes in a very personal way. One missionary struggled with the decision to go on his mission. He didn't think he had anything special to offer. Little did he know that there were people who were waiting for his unique personality and gifts. At the end of his mission he said, "Everyone needs to hear the gospel, but I found people who needed to hear it from me and perhaps would not have listened to someone else in the same way. I've found people who needed to hear my voice."

The best way to lift another is to help that person move closer to the Savior through embracing His restored gospel and learning to live the commandments. Commandments have been given to lift us and not to put us down.

For example, anyone who has never had to get a visa to live in a foreign country has missed out on a crazy journal entry. Russell felt very blessed when after a long delay, his visa to enter Spain finally arrived. There are times when missionaries are denied visas and have to be reassigned.

I will never forget the day I had to renew visas so our family could stay in Chile. We woke up at 5:00 A.M. to get downtown to the building where we were to go. After waiting in a line for a long while, we reached the counter, only to be told we were in the wrong line. In the next line, I went right to the front to make sure it was the right place. "Yes," the man said. "This is the line where you need to be." So I went to the back of the line with the family, and we all waited patiently. When our turn finally came several hours later, the same man checked our papers and said—you guessed it—"You're in the wrong line." This went on all day. We got shuffled from building to building, line to line, and paid fee after fee until finally being told the place was closing and we would have to wake up the next day at 5:00 A.M. to start all over again.

We may not like the regulations that governments have, but we all accept those regulations. Why is it so hard then for people to accept that God also requires something of us? One frustrated missionary wrote to me: "We tried to commit a woman to baptism and she said straight out she would rather keep drinking. No matter how many times I see people reject baptism for some weak excuse, it will never cease to amaze me. Helloooo! Do you hear yourself? Drinking or God? Is it really that hard? I guess for some people it is. It is a matter of perspective. Most kids will take 100 pesos right now rather than a thousand tomorrow. Call it maturity, wisdom, common sense, or whatever. Why can't we get people to have a long-term perspective and show some maturity when it comes to their lives?"

He is not the only missionary who has ever felt that way. Another elder said it like this: "I'm getting tired of people just being comfortable and not reaching out for more. They are missing so many blessings. With just the smallest effort, they could reach their potentials. I know the Lord probably feels the same about me some-times, but it is so hard seeing people CTW (choose the wrong!)."

In Chile the missionaries hear a phrase often: *a mi manera*. It means "my way" and people are always saying that's how they want to follow God. Another common response from people is, "I am a spiritual person, but not religious." Others say, "I believe in God but not in organized religion." No matter what they say in whatever lan-guage it always translates into *I don't want God to have any requirements. I don't want to wake up early, wait in any lines, or pay any fees.* What they fail to understand is that while the laws imposed by governments may or may not be for our best good, the laws of God are always given for our benefit and with our best interest in mind (see Alma 41:8).

One missionary said, "It's frustrating to be offering something so important and not have anyone want it. The restored gospel is for everyone. It's not like a product in a store and people can buy or not buy. It is essential. It's not a product we are selling, it is the way of life and salvation and everyone needs it. They may not know it, but they do. It is as necessary as air and water."

Another elder insightfully wrote, "So many think that having a belief in the existence of God is enough, but it isn't. We can't return to God without coming to Christ. And in the same way, there is no way we can come to Christ without coming to his Church."

One sister missionary observed, "There is no better feeling in the world than to help people connect with God. I have taught people to pray who have never prayed before. One lady cried and said, 'That's the first time I've ever talked to God.' It felt good to see her make the connection that makes all the difference in this life."

LEARNING

The prophecy in Ezekiel 47 talks about healing and life-giving waters that flow out to change the world. However, Ezekiel is also instructed to wade into the water. The first time he enters it, "the waters were to the ankles." Then he walks down the bank a little farther and wades in again. This time "the waters were to the knees." He is told to continue and next finds "the waters were to the loins." Finally, Ezekiel speaks of waters into which he could immerse himself. "It was a river that I could not pass over: for the waters were risen, waters to swim in" (Ezekiel 47:3–5).

Though this prophecy refers to returning again and again to the temple and learning to value the symbolism there, it also says a lot about gospel learning in general. On missions many young people find their understandings of spiritual things deepen. They are no longer satisfied with just getting their feet wet. They desire to dive in headfirst to reading, studying, and making meaning of life's experiences. They go beyond wading in the things of the Spirit and the words of living prophets to immersing themselves completely and finding "waters to swim in."

One missionary said, "On the mission I have learned to love two things I didn't like much before: tomatoes and general conference. Now I can't get enough of either one!"

Listen to what other missionaries learned as they swam instead of waded:

An elder: "The Church has always been the most solid and consistent thing in my crazy life. I can always count on it. It's hard sometimes, but I have learned I can do hard things."

Another elder: "The desires are what make a person. People usually get what they want. The problem is they usually don't want what they should or they don't want it long enough."

A sister missionary: "You don't always see the fruits of your labors, but then some small thing happens and you know you were in the right place at the right time."

An elder: "I learned that Christ is more than amazing, more than intelligent, more than incredible. Not only are there no words to adequately describe him, there are no words to describe how I feel about him. I always knew he was my Savior, but now I understand more about what that means."

Another elder: "I grew more spiritually on my mission than I had my entire life before. I can count the books I read before my mission on one hand. Now I honestly can't stop reading."

Another elder: "My outlook on everything has changed. I simply don't think the same as I did before (and that's good). What was important to me then isn't that important and what I didn't care much about has become my priority."

Another elder: "I always wanted to see Christ. I always felt like that would be the ultimate, but if you think about it, everyone will see him one day. Just seeing him doesn't change a person. The goal isn't just to see him, but to be like him. That happens over time as the Spirit works with us and molds us. The ultimate is not seeing him, but Him seeing his countenance in us. . . . My children and my children's children will hear about the people I have met on my mission and the difference that came into my life."

A sister: "The mission has been like an onion—sometimes it made me cry, but it was worth it because of the flavor it added to my life."

An elder: "In the Bible you read of how Christ took a few loaves of bread and fishes and used them to feed thousands. I think that is what he does with missions. He takes a few elders and sisters and then multiplies our efforts to bless thousands."

A hardworking elder: "I've learned that if we don't sweat in the sector we will never get wet in the baptismal font. I've learned to work my heart out for a good cause."

Another elder: "I always knew I should go on a mission, but I never dreamed of all I would become on a mission."

Such profound lessons don't come easily. The mission is a hard teacher but, just like in school, the hard teachers usually teach us the most. The easy teachers are fun but rarely as effective. Students also have to take responsibility for their own learning. In the Old Testament prophecy, Ezekiel had to do his part. He had to enter the river over and over again before he saw the benefits he desired.

One parent wrote to me and said, "Our son has grown five years in two." It was true. Why? As you look at rings on a tree you can see some years in which the tree didn't grow much and other years in which it did indeed grow "five years in two." In trees, the difference is water. For missionaries it is also water—tears that have fallen during hard times, the water in a baptismal font that changes both missionary and convert, the sacrament water that is finally taken sincerely and seriously. Maybe it is the water in Ezekiel's prophecy that has not only reached out to touch us with life and healing, but has also invited us in for a swim. Living water affects our growth rings as well. In the same way a river carved the Grand Canyon over time, we let the living waters wash over us and shape us into something spectacular.

WHAT I TRIED

In this chapter we have written a lot about the river in Ezekiel. I guess now is when I had better remind parents that we can't teach a kid to swim by just throwing him in the deep water unprepared. In the scripture, Ezekiel talks about a man with the line in his hand who measured a thousand cubits over and over again. That is our part. We have to do the little things over and over.

We must start a savings account for our future missionaries and help them contribute to it. We need to refer often to, "When you go on your mission . . ." and teach them to frequently sing "I Hope They Call Me on a Mission" from an early age. We need to teach them to sincerely pray for missionaries and for our future missionaries. We can dedicate our monthly fast to missionaries in the ward, missionaries in the MTC, and even returned missionaries who are making the difficult transition home. We need to greet missionaries, feed missionaries, and invite them to teach in our homes. This not only supports the missionaries in their work, but also sends powerful and positive messages to our children about the importance of missions.

I know, I know. We also need to be trustworthy, loyal, helpful, friendly, courteous . . . the list is endless. All these "little things" add up until they constitute a huge investment of time, energy, money, and focus. All I can say is that I'm glad my folks did it for my brothers and me. I'm grateful my own children have responded to our efforts.

And when children don't respond, when they have had wonderful examples and consistent teaching and still turn their backs on what they know and choose to learn the hard way, we can't give up. They break the rules. They break the law. They break our hearts. At such low moments, we can never underestimate the power of a prayerful parent (see Mosiah 27:14). There are times when the only thing left to do is to pour out our hearts to Heavenly Father, who shares our parental concerns and responsibilities.

RUSSELL'S RESPONSE

Dad writes about the importance of having a missionary savings account. I remember having a bank shaped like a big crayon in my room into which I would place money for my mission. Then when Dad needed cash he would raid my savings. When we finally went to the bank to open an official account there were sure a lot of notes from my dad in that crayon bank that said, "I owe you." I made him pay back every cent!

Dad also writes about fasting. In all honesty, that hasn't always been a strong point in the Wilcox home. Saturday lunch gets eaten pretty late on the first weekend of every month and Sunday lunch comes as early as possible. I was the worst offender growing up. I remember hurrying downstairs and eating breakfast cereal before my parents could remind me it was fast Sunday. It's pretty sad when you actually plan to forget!

As I have grown and my understanding and appreciation for fasting have increased, I've realized that it can be a powerful tool in preparing children to stay on missions. I can't think of anything that teaches mind over matter or spirit over body like fasting. Each time we fast we are reminding our bodies who is in control. That is the exact ability missionaries need when they start toying with the idea of giving up and going home. When a missionary feels his spirit is willing but his flesh is weak, fasting can strengthen the spirit and remind that weak flesh who is in charge.

Our family friend Hal Jones had a powerful impact on our lives. When I was very young he told me, "You gotta do what you don't want to do to get what you want to get." I can't even tell you how many times I have reminded myself of those words as I have worked toward a goal or tried to endure to the end. Sometimes I even hate those words because I don't want them to be true, but they are. Especially in the mission field, you often have to do what you don't want to do to get what you want to get. Nothing teaches that principle better than fasting.

KEYS TO ACTION

What Can We Do FOR Young People?

Making a commitment to be baptized is huge. But frequently and confidently referring to an investigator's baptism makes it seem less daunting and not such a strange or impossible goal. The same thing is true of parents and leaders talking with young people about missions. If the subject is brought up often and it is simply assumed that a young man is going to serve, it will not seem so foreign as the actual date approaches.

Of all the little things we can do to encourage missions, perhaps the most effective incentive comes from telling and hearing stories. I remember listening to my brothers talking about their missionary experiences. I remember being especially motivated by the stories of my older cousin, Dale Allred. Dale had served in Sweden, and he was so enthusiastic about that mission that he had me thinking that a call to any other mission just wouldn't do. I didn't get called to Sweden, but I did carry Dale's enthusiasm for missionary work all through my own mission in Chile. Another cousin, Bill Wilcox, actually served in Chile a few years before me. As Bill would write to me in the mission field and share stories of his experiences and recall the people he had known it was especially meaningful because I was serving in some of the same areas and working with similar people. The mission experiences we had in common created a close connection and bond between us.

As he was growing up, Russell was impressed by stories told by returned missionaries who taught him in Sunday School classes and in priesthood quorums. Seminary teachers and EFY speakers also had an impact. Their accounts of their missionary experiences sank into his heart and made lasting impressions. Each story spoke of possibilities in his life. Each story gave him ideas for dealing with similar situations. Each story validated him and assured him he was not alone in his thoughts, feelings, and desires.

There is a power in storytelling that goes beyond our understanding. Scriptures contain stories. Family histories are full of stories. Effective teachers use stories to illustrate their points. Even in the temple, where we learn the lessons of eternity, much of what is presented comes to us in the form of a story.

We're not just talking about family stories, as fun as they are to hear. (The Wilcox kids love hearing about when their mom went to a formal dance in overalls and pigtails or when she toilet-papered a police station.) Recounting missionary experiences invites the Holy Spirit into the conversation. Listening to them can stir a young man's soul and help instill in him a desire to experience these things himself. The events of our missions may seem less than spectacular to us, but they often have a powerful effect on a child who listens in wide-eyed wonder.

It's hard to imagine, but I suppose there are some moms and dads who consciously or subconsciously resist the idea of their sons going on a mission. They don't want to tell stories that might encourage them because perhaps Mom can't bear the thought of separation, or maybe Dad is reluctant to give up his fishing buddy. These parents need to consider that rather than cutting short their relationship with their son, a mission can actually extend it.

When a young man gets to be nineteen years old, he is usually well into the process of establishing his independence. He may be physically present, but at that age he is not likely to voluntarily and completely share his deepest feelings with Mom or Dad. He probably won't express appreciation freely or come home from a date and sit on the side of his folks' bed, excited to share the events of the evening. Because of his growing independence, he is also not likely to share the emotions he is experiencing.

But when he goes on a mission and he begins to reflect on the comforts of home, the memories of his mother's selfless service, or the ease of his former life, something awakens in him. Letters and e-mails begin to be filled with expressions of love and appreciation for things previously taken for granted, along with descriptions of the challenge of adapting to a new culture, his companion, and a demanding schedule. As his testimony grows and he begins to relish spiritual experiences, he will also share the wonder of these moments with his parents. He now has his own mission stories to share.

At a time in his life when communication with home would normally be largely tailing off, missions allow for it to be reestablished and extended. Through letters and e-mails—and even those priceless twice-a-year phone calls at Christmas and Mother's Day—the missionary willingly shares tender feelings and describes spiritual experiences he would otherwise never have talked about. That is what parents of a missionary refer to when they say they can't wait to hear from their son. Now instead of telling the stories, they are listening to them. This enriched communication and strengthened relationship is one of the wonderful perks of having a child serve a mission.

What Can We Do WITH Young People?

When I was teaching elementary school and a child would say, "I'm sick. I want to call home," I wouldn't always immediately agree. Unless the child was obviously ill, I would often respond by saying, "Hang in there for fifteen minutes, and then we will go make the call." Often the child would forget he was feeling ill. He would become involved in the class activities and never remember he wanted to call home. If, after fifteen minutes, he was still feeling sick, the call would be made.

With regard to a mission, a young man sometimes needs to take a little time to wade in the river before plunging fully in. When declarations are made, such as, "I'm not going on a mission," or, "I'm going home," they are usually made in a particularly hard or low moment.

As a mission president, I took a page from my experience teaching school. After hearing a particular missionary's long list of reasons why he or she needed to go home, instead of immediately agreeing, I would say, "Let's wait a few days and see how you're feeling," or "Let's try this or that and make this or that change and then see how you are feeling about it." Usually, just as did the elementary school students, the missionary would become involved in the work and forget his desire to leave.

However, now and then the request would still surface. Then I would try to buy more time. Knowing that the young man's parents, his bishop, and his stake president would likely encourage the young man to stay, I would suggest he call them to discuss the situation.

I was told the following story by a stake president I know: A young man who had planned all his life to serve a mission and had departed for the mission field with great enthusiasm, somehow lost his courage. After just a couple of weeks in the mission, he began phoning his parents, begging for their permission to come home. They didn't want that, and in an attempt to buy some time, said that they couldn't authorize his coming home and that he would have to call his stake president.

The young man was halfway around the world from his home, and his midday call from where he was assigned came in the middle of the night to the sleeping stake president, who listened patiently for several minutes to the unhappy missionary's complaints and whining. Then the president simply said, "Lance, I don't know anyone here who wants to see you." Stunned by that dose of reality, the young man paused for a moment, then said, "Oh," and hung up. He ended up staying in the mission field and had a successful mission.

If one of my missionaries could still not be persuaded to remain on his mission, I would attempt to buy even more time by asking him to wait until the regularly scheduled times for departures rather than disrupting the schedule of the whole mission. Sometimes I would have the missionary come and stay at the mission home for a while so Sister Wilcox and I could provide lots of personal attention and love. In many cases, time was a helpful friend.

Still, there was one elder who was determined to go home no matter what anyone might counsel. I told him that a group was leaving at the end of the week and said that if his feelings hadn't changed by then I would send him home with the departing missionaries.

The day of the final interviews arrived, and I sat and listened as each departing missionary shared with me how much his or her mission had meant. It was inspiring to hear their testimonies, plans, and goals, and I had the privilege of giving each a blessing. Finally, after all the final interviews were over, I sat down with the elder who wanted to go home early. Once again, I listened to all his reasons, but they sounded so hollow after the glowing testimonies I had just heard. Finally, I said, "I'm sorry. You caught me on the wrong day! There is no way I am going to let you miss what all these other missionaries have gained. I can't in good conscience send you home half-baked." We then set some new goals, made some new plans, and I gave him a blessing.

Wonderful things started to happen. Slowly but surely all the reasons that had seemed so compelling for him to go home began to fade. He got involved using his talents in the work, and he received assignments that kept him working so hard he had little time to think of anything else. He began to make friends in the mission and to feel more confident with his Spanish. He began to have success, and he completed his mission not just flying, but soaring. At the time of his honorable release, he wrote, "President: I remember when you told me I caught you on the wrong day and how mad I was at you for not giving me my way. I could see exactly what you were doing as you kept stretching the time out, and it really bugged me. Now, all I can say is thanks. Whatever you did worked. I love my mission and can't even imagine what would have happened in my life had I gone home. Thanks."

We wish all stories could have such happy endings. There are some missionaries who do decide to leave and cannot be dissuaded. There are some who have to leave early due to health problems. But their stories don't end because their missions end. There are still many happy endings that can and will come in time. That's the point. Change often takes time.

What Can Young People Do BY THEMSELVES?

Journals are valuable places to record our experiences, but they are also wonderful tools that help us create, recognize, and shape our thoughts and feelings. If we are wise, we don't wait to write until we have something to say. Most of the time, it is in the act of writing that we realize what we have to say.

Someone asked me once why I am such an avid journal writer. I said, "It's cheaper than counseling!" Truly, a journal does provide a safe place where we can explore our innermost feelings and deal with them appropriately. Journals validate our feelings as well as our observations, ideas, and dreams. Russell must have picked up journal writing from his dad because he has always kept a regular journal. He found it especially useful on his mission.

We sometimes tell ourselves that we keep our journals for our posterity. Well, maybe some great-grandchild will break both legs and be desperate enough for something to do that he'll pull out our dust-covered journals. But the remote possibility of such an event in the future has never been motivation enough for Russell or me to keep our journals. In our lives, we had to discover that writing in a journal is valuable for us—whether or not our grandchildren ever read them.

Writing is an important form of communication, but that is scarcely its major value. Like shooting baskets all alone in your driveway, writing does not require an audience beyond yourself to be worthwhile or enjoyable.

When Grandpa and Grandma Gunnell were moving to Colorado, a tragic moving-van fire destroyed all their belongings, including family photograph albums and personal journals. One well-meaning friend lamented, "All that work for nothing!"

Grandma responded: "The process we went through writing our journals can never be burned. Every hour we spent on those books helped to make us the people we have become." Like Grandma Gunnell, Russell and I have found our personal journals an ideal environment in which to "become." It is a perfect place for us to live, laugh, love, lift, and learn.

Part Two:

STUDY

▲ ▲ ▲

"The study habits you develop as a missionary will bless you personally and help those you teach grow in their faith in the Savior."

Preach My Gospel, *17*

3

▲ ▲ ▲

SUITS WITH WORN-OUT KNEES

On Russell's mission in Spain, there were those who would say, "Mormons are not Christians."

Russell would respond, "Of course we are. The name of the Church is the Church of Jesus Christ."

Then some would counter, "But you believe in a different Christ."

Russell would say, "We believe in the exact same Christ that you do. We just know him better." How could Russell make such a bold claim? Because we have additional scripture and the words of living apostles and prophets that testify of Christ and help us come to know him. The view of most Christians is limited to the Bible only. While we appreciate, use, and love the Bible, our view is broader and more comprehensive because of additional sources that teach us more about the Savior.

It is one thing to *believe* in Jesus. It is another thing to *know* him. Jesus prayed to the Father, saying, "And this is life eternal, that they might *know* thee the only true God, and Jesus Christ, whom thou hast sent" (John 17:3; emphasis added).

When one elder arrived in his mission he had already lost a lot of weight in order to meet the requirements to serve. Over the next few months, he continued shedding the pounds. Pretty soon he needed to take his suits to a local shop to have them altered. The woman at the shop, who was not a member of the Church, could see the elder was thinner, so she understood why the coat and pants needed to be taken in, but she couldn't figure out why the knees on the pants were almost worn through.

Worn-out knees were just one of the indications that Elder Thomas was changing spiritually as well as physically. His waistline was shrinking, but his testimony was growing.

Like Elder Thomas, many missionaries become more fit on their missions. They also acquire improved study habits, work habits, and people skills. Many live among those of different cultures and some learn foreign languages. But such benefits could be gained at school or on a sports team. We can sign up for a study abroad program and learn about cultures and languages. The one thing a missionary can do on a mission that he can't do nearly as well elsewhere is draw closer to the Savior. With a focus on the Savior, all the studying, learning, working, and teaching become profoundly more significant and enduring.

One capable sister missionary wrote, "If there is anything I'm learning on my mission it is to know God and Jesus Christ and to trust them. Because of Christ no problem is left without a solution, no pain without relief, no sickness without healing. The scriptures say Christ has healing in his wings. I have felt him lift me with those wings of healing and now Christ's healing power has given me wings."

Elder Rojas said, "I always had faith in Christ, but it was a Christ who was far away. Now I have faith in the same Christ, but I am much closer to him."

These missionaries have come to appreciate what Jesus taught when he said, "I am the way, the truth, and the life" (John 14:6). President Ezra Taft Benson testified, "When you choose to follow Christ, you choose . . . the right way, the saving truth, the abundant life."[10]

THE RIGHT WAY

In Joseph Smith's day, people were concerned about which of all the churches was right. Now it seems as though we are lucky to have people express any interest in religion at all. Those who are not completely apathetic seem content with the view that "All churches are the same," or, "It doesn't matter which church becomes your spiritual home as long as you are a good person." Although such reasoning seems about the same as inviting everyone to write his or her own instruction manual for assembling the space shuttle, it's amazing how many people buy into it.

It is baffling how people can clearly see that all hospitals, schools, stores, and countries are *not* the same and yet claim that all religions *are* the same. To recognize that one school or hospital is better than another seems the mark of an intelligent and informed person. However, to claim one church is better than another is viewed as intolerant or not "politically correct."

Regardless of people's viewpoints and opinions, truth is truth (see Alma 41:8). Many may try to cover the clock, but they can't change the time. People can vote on which direction is north, but they can't change the North Star. They may be looking for an easy way out, but in the end they will discover that happiness and peace come from conforming our lives to truth and not trying to bend truth to fit our current, selfish desires. Noah's ark held only eight people, but in the end they were right and the all rest were wrong. That may sound harsh, but as relative as the truth may have seemed before the rain started falling, in the end it was absolute truth that mattered.

Contrary to popular belief, all roads do *not* lead to God. However, they do lead someplace, and that is to a Mormon baptismal font. Whether in this life or the next, everyone will ultimately have the opportunity to receive essential ordinances. Then, those who accept them will truly be on the one road that leads to God.

During Russell's mission he explained this principle to an investigator by asking for his phone number. He then pretended to call him, changing one of the numbers. "Am I going to reach you?" he asked.

"Of course not," came the reply.

Russell said, "Just as there is a right way to call you, there is also a right way to reach God. Our job is not to invent numbers that please us, but learn and dial the numbers that will get us through."

One man had been investigating the Church with his family for a long time. His family all joined and the man attended meetings and activities, but he saw no need to commit. The missionaries challenged him to listen again to the lessons. He said, "Elders, I've heard them so many times I could probably give them to you." They challenged him to read in the Book of Mormon. He said, "I'm in Mosiah 4 on my third time through."

Finally, on a day when the family had provided dinner for the missionaries, one of the elders pulled the father aside and said, "You know that Satan has convinced a lot of people in this world that there is no God."

"Not me," said the man. "I know there is a God."

The elder continued, "Satan has convinced a lot of people who know there is a God that there is no true church—that any church will do."

"Not me," said the man. "I know this is the true Church."

Then, with quiet conviction and sincere caring, the elder continued, "Satan has convinced a lot of people who know this is the true Church that there is no hurry—tomorrow will be soon enough" (see 2 Nephi 28:21–25).

The man sat in silence as the missionary stood to leave. As the elder was putting on his coat, he said to the man, "The way I figure, if Satan can convince us there is no rush, then we really aren't any better off than those who believe there is no God and no such thing as truth."

Two days later the man requested his baptismal interview.

THE SAVING TRUTH

One accusation that missionaries hear a lot is that The Church of Jesus Christ of Latter-day Saints is not a legitimate church but only a sect or a cult. People use those words because they have a negative connotation, but many who use them don't have a clear understanding of what they mean.

A sect is a minority religious body that adheres to a distinctive doctrine. Sects are usually exclusive and teach that they have the only way to be saved. Mormons do have a unique set of doctrines and proclaim the Church to be the only true church. However, the same could be said of all Christians. Christian doctrine is different from other world religions, and Christians claim that the only way to be saved is by accepting Jesus. If Mormonism is a sect, then by the same definition, so is all of Christianity. Latter-day Saints are far from being exclusive. On the contrary, we bend over backward to share what we have with everyone—including those who have already passed away. We do not testify of the "only true Church" in the spirit of superiority or exclusion, but rather in a spirit of invitation (see Alma 5:62).

A cult, like a sect, is a minority religious body with nontraditional views, including great devotion to a leader who represents the ideal pattern to follow. Falsely believing that Latter-day Saints idealize or even worship Joseph Smith, some describe Mormonism as a cult. Latter-day Saints do not worship Joseph Smith. We respect him as one who was called by the Lord to be the prophet of this dispensation, but we know the church Joseph Smith organized is the Church of Jesus Christ. It was the Lord who authorized and directed its organization, and it is Christ who leads the Church. Christ is our ideal. If that makes us a cult, then by the same definition, all of Christianity is a cult for patterning itself after the Savior.

Cults are sometimes associated with secret ceremonies. Perhaps a misconception of what goes on in our temples is the basis of some claims that Mormons are cultists. Those who take the time to investigate realize that temple ordinances are not secret. Like a university, the doors are open to all who will first prepare themselves and pass the entrance exam. Universities do not restrict admissions in order to hide the knowledge they possess. On the contrary, they are anxious to share knowledge with all who seek it. The entrance requirements at universities are not used to keep people out, but rather to ensure that those who enter are prepared and likely to succeed. In the same manner, LDS temples are open to all who meet the qualifications to enter. If having a temple entrance requirement makes Mormonism a secret cult, then all major universities would also have to be called cults.

Though the world variously defines our church as a sect, a cult, or even a new religion, we define ourselves as custodians of truth—the same truth that was had by Adam, Enoch, Noah, Abraham, and Moses. We have and teach the same truth taught by Jesus when he was on the earth and his apostles after him. That truth was lost during dark years of apostasy, but it was restored again in its fulness through the revelations given to Joseph Smith and others (see D&C 1:17–24).

Some textbooks call Joseph Smith the "first Mormon." The same textbooks call Christ the "first Christian." We don't agree with either statement. It was actually Adam and Eve who were the first members of Christ's Church on this earth (see Moses 6:65–68). There were many who were baptized into that Church long before Jesus was born into mortality (see Mosiah 18). Jesus himself was baptized into his own Church (see Matthew 3:16). What the world calls *Mormonism* is not a sect, cult, or new religion. It is a restoration of truth that is as old as the world and beyond.

President Spencer W. Kimball testified:

> This Church of Jesus Christ (nicknamed *Mormon*) is the 'only true and living church.' . . . This is an absolute truth. It cannot be disproved. It is as true as the near-spherical shape of the earth, and as gravity; as true as the shining of the sun—as positive as the truth that we live. Most of the world disbelieves it; ministers attempt to disprove it; intellectuals think to rationalize it out of existence; but when all the people of the world are dead . . . the truth will go forward—the Church will continue triumphant.[11]

In Spain, Russell and his companion taught a man who didn't believe in God. The elders explained that a serious study of the Book of Mormon could change his views. The man said, "You can't prove God exists."

Russell said, "And you can't prove he doesn't."

The man said, "I wouldn't even if I could. You are so happy with your belief. I wouldn't want to ruin that for you."

Russell said, "I'm glad you recognize that we are happy, but that is a result of knowledge and not of ignorance. I'm not happy because I am in some little bubble—a pretend world of my own creating, sheltered from harsh reality by my fantasies. No way! My happiness is because I know the truth and I choose to live according to that knowledge. I know that God is real and he loves me. You can know, too. We don't have to just guess or wonder. We don't have to just hope or cross our fingers. We can know."

THE ABUNDANT LIFE

Jesus said, "I am come that they might have life, and that they might have it more abundantly" (John 10:10). President Spencer W. Kimball taught:

How foolish would be the enslaved Israelite who was born in slavery and had never known anything but slavery to say to himself, "This is life. There is nothing better than this. Here I get my belly full daily and a fair space in which to sleep." How short-sighted he would be to prefer such status when he is told that across the sea and across the desert a promised land awaits where he can be free and well-fed, be master of his own destinies, and have leisure, culture, growth, and all one's heart could rightfully desire.[12]

The Church offers a healthy lifestyle, a focus on education, an international network of contacts and friends, a strong support system, and a sense of community. The Church boasts of promoting positive and successful marriages and strong families and of having many prominent members who are positive role models for others. The benefits of belonging can add up. Still, few come into the Church because of research studies showing that Mormons live longer or because we have higher levels of education than the general public. They enter because they gain a spiritual witness of the Savior. That testimony is what leads them to the abundant life.

One missionary said, "I would be incomplete without the gospel. If the Church were taken away from me it would tear me apart."

Another missionary, a sister, wrote, "I read in *Preach My Gospel* that once you come to understand the Atonement, your desire to share the gospel will increase. It doesn't just mean the more you read books and articles about it or study it. It means the more you experience the power of the Atonement in your own life. . . . These last few months I have felt a huge weight, but lately I've been feeling that weight being lifted. I have felt closer to my Savior than ever before. I have felt him literally lifting this burden off of me and giving me peace and joy, and now I have a whole new desire to share the gospel. Nothing has changed around me. It's just that I'm letting the Savior in, and he is changing me."

Elder David A. Bednar of the Quorum of the Twelve states, "Coming unto Christ is not a single event with a fixed point of beginning or ending; rather, it is a process that develops and deepens during a lifetime."[13]

To become more Christlike and to help others do the same is the driving force behind everything that happens in a mission. It is the force that changes chores to challenges, obligations to opportunities, and endurance to enjoyment. It is the force that changes us from bad to good, from good to better, and from better to truly "having the image of God engraven upon [our] countenances" (Alma 5:19).

Jesus is not *a* way, *a* truth, and *a pretty nice* life. He is *the* way, *the* truth, and *the* life. Years ago the official logo of the Church was redesigned to emphasize the name of Jesus Christ, which became the center of the design and was made much larger than the surrounding words. This is exactly as it should be. However, perhaps there is another word in the name of the Church that also deserves emphasis—not in the logo, but in our understanding. The word is *The*. This is not *A* true church, *another* true church, a *good* church, or one of many equally good paths that can be chosen and followed. This is *The* Church of Jesus Christ.

The scriptures promise that one day every knee shall bow and every tongue confess that Jesus is the Christ (see Romans 14:11; D&C 76:110). As arrogant as it may sound to some, I am convinced that that confession will also include the recognition that the Mormons were truly God's authorized agents, humbly attempting to fulfill the commission given them by the Savior: "Go ye therefore, and teach all nations, baptizing them in the name of the Father, and of the Son, and of the Holy Ghost: Teaching them to observe all things whatsoever I have commanded you" (Matthew 28:19–20). That will be a validating day for missionaries who have faced so much ridicule and rejection.

Though there are millions and millions of Christians in the

world, and though many of them love and follow the Savior with all sincerity, the members of The Church of Jesus Christ are the only Christians in the world who do not simply follow Christ. We are led by him in the same way he has always led his people—through living prophets and apostles. That knowledge sets our faith and testimonies apart. We hope it will set our motives and behavior apart.

WHAT I TRIED

In an effort to learn more about the Savior, we have tried various approaches to having family scripture study through the years. Some attempts have been more successful than others. We have tried having everyone follow along in their own copies, and then we tried just having them listen as Debi or I read. We have tried discussing the scriptures and reading commentaries. Then we tried just reading them without interruption. We have tried reading in the morning and also during dinner. We even tried reading to the kids in their car pool on the way to school each morning. We still don't have the "ideal" way to suggest since it seems to have changed a lot as our children grew through different ages and stages. Perhaps the best thing we did was be consistent. We missed more days than we should have and always seemed to struggle more on weekends and in the summer when the kids were out of their routine. Still, even with all the slipups, our children knew family scripture reading would never go away for good. The consistency sent the message to the children that we valued the scriptures.

I remember once when the children were young my wife and I got quite discouraged, and I said, "They aren't getting anything out of this at all." Debi said, "At least they are hearing the sounds of the scriptures and becoming familiar with the language." She was right. Just as taking young children to church is valuable even when meetings hit right during naptimes, regular scripture reading teaches an essential routine, habit, and language.

RUSSELL'S RESPONSE

Since returning from my mission, every morning when I wake up and start to get ready, I usually hear my mom listening to scriptures on tape as she gets ready herself. When I go downstairs for breakfast, I usually am met by my dad's voice reading the Book of Mormon to my younger brother and sister before they go to school. It's similar to the morning routine we had when I was growing up. The difference is that now I realize the value of it.

At one time my dad decided he could get a little extra scripture study in if he read as he "walked on the treadmill." I put that in quotations because more often than not I caught him marking his scriptures as the machine continued to run on its own. Good exercise, Dad! Now he listens to the Book of Mormon in Spanish while he walks.

I remember when we drove in a car pool to high school in the mornings. Some of the parents played music while we drove and others asked occasional questions or just let us sit in silence. Not my dad. No, he had us take turns reading out of the scriptures. At first I felt a little embarrassed. I figured that the other teenagers we picked up in the morning would rebel and decide to walk to school. But actually they started to look forward to the days when my dad drove. Sure, we all complained outwardly and had to give him a hard time, but inwardly we liked it.

My dad was right about my not getting much out of the scriptures when I was younger. I have to confess I tuned out a lot. I was usually more interested in reading the back of the cereal box than listening to the scriptures. However, my mom was right, too. Just by being there and being exposed to the words and language, I became comfortable with them. The *thees* and the *thous* don't lose me. I don't necessarily remember the specifics of what we read, but I remember reading. The scriptures became part of my life and now I love them and study them regularly. I will probably end up reading them to my own kids when I'm in charge of the car pool!

KEYS TO ACTION

What Can We Do FOR Young People?

It is said that a person can tell what is truly in our hearts by examining what is hanging on our walls. While such a generalization cannot always be supported, it is surprising how often we have found that to be the case. A friend who loves cars has photos of them all over his walls. Another friend who loves jazz music has posters of famous performers all over his bedroom. Someone who loves animals can't seem to resist hanging up a calendar showing pictures of kittens and puppies.

Can someone coming into our home find pictures of the Savior, the prophets, and the temples? Could that visitor locate a picture of our family or something representing our missions?

One newcomer to Utah who was not a member of the Church became friends with her neighbors and was welcomed into their homes. In one house she saw a picture of a smiling elderly man and assumed it must be a photo of a grandfather. Then she saw the same smiling man in the homes of all her neighbors. She wondered, *How can all these people have the same grandfather?* When she finally asked her friends about it they had a good laugh and explained that this beloved grandfather was the prophet.

It is probably impossible to overstate the influence the artwork and photographs we display in our homes has on our young people. They see these things every day and can't help being affected by them.

What Can We Do WITH Young People?

Encourage seminary attendance. It is always disheartening to hear about LDS parents who tell their high schoolers that they would be better off taking another advanced placement course rather than "wasting time" in seminary. These parents may have their children's short-term interests in mind, but they are overlooking their long-term needs.

Sometimes encouraging seminary attendance means waking up early with our children. Other times it means driving them to school. It may mean helping to teach the classes. Whatever it takes, seminary needs to be a priority. Not only does seminary provide a welcome daily respite from the worldliness that permeates our schools, but it also plants noble thoughts, an understanding of the scriptures, and a love of the Savior in a young person's heart. It helps, too, that the teachers talk about the importance of serving a mission and testify of their own treasured experiences in having served.

When our family moved to New Zealand, it was the first time Russell attended school where there was no released-time seminary. When the young people in the ward told him how early they met in the morning, he about passed out. He said, "No way! I'm not going!"

However, the class was small enough that his absence was very noticeable. He soon felt just enough positive peer pressure that he decided to give it a try. Later, he wouldn't have missed it for anything. Attending that early morning seminary class in Auckland became the highlight of his day and ended up being a major turning point in his life.

Seminary is the place where good Mormon kids from good Mormon families can finally figure out the difference between *pilgrims* and *pioneers*. They can finally realize President Lincoln was not a prophet and that Brigham Young was not the president of the country. It is where they learn that Samuel the Lamanite is not in the Bible and that Moses came after Noah. In many cases, seminary is where young people first gain a respect for both the complexity and simplicity of the gospel. One young man said, "I used to feel passion for sports and my drums, but thanks to my great seminary teacher, I'm now starting to feel that same kind of passion for the gospel."

What Can Young People Do BY THEMSELVES?

Now and then a missionary at the MTC will say to Russell, "I'm just not getting anything out of my scripture reading. I read a whole page and then either fall asleep or find my mind has wandered to something else."

Two ways to engage more in reading are to mark scriptures and to keep a scripture journal. Some think the only reason to mark scriptures is to help us find them again, but that's only one of the benefits. As we mark them it also helps us stay focused on what we are reading and helps us internalize, personalize, and remember the messages. Some mark favorite passages. Others mark references to Christ or a particular topic. Still others mark scriptures that link to other scriptures. Lots of people will have suggestions about what has worked best for them. Yellow, green, red—whatever works. Pencils, pens, markers, special stickers—whatever works. As we keep our hands busy, we keep our minds focused.

Study journals are also important in making personal scripture study more meaningful. Some write summaries and ideas for future lessons or talks. Others write personal connections and memories or questions about phrases they don't yet understand. As with marking scriptures, the main thing is that we are engaged.

As we read we take what is outside of us and put it inside. When we write we take what's inside our minds and bring it out. That creates a needed balance in our learning and in our living. Consider the sharing of testimonies. We can listen to testimonies, yet we have a totally different experience when we are the ones doing the speaking and having to find words for those difficult-to-express feelings. The Spirit can confirm the words of another, but when the Spirit bears witness of our own words, it is life changing.

We commonly hear a teacher or speaker in church say, "I think I am the one who will get the most out of this lesson or talk." It's true. We always benefit from being in the position of having to give as well as receive. That is part of the wisdom of sending young people on missions where they become the teachers. They may have learned the gospel before, but when they have to teach it, they suddenly find themselves learning it in a much deeper and more meaningful way. The same wisdom applies in keeping study journals, where readers suddenly become writers. The journal provides a safe place for us to record thoughts, feelings, insights, and inspirations and—interestingly enough—as we record them, we usually end up having more of them. One missionary wrote, "I have finally been writing regularly in my study journal and since then I've been receiving more personal revelation. I should have started sooner."

4

▲ ▲ ▲

WHAT TO DO WHEN THEY
SAY IT'S <u>NOT</u> TRUE

"I looked up *Mormon* on the Internet and found all kinds of weird stuff," said one recent convert. Another said, "People I didn't even know at work were passing me pages of anti-Mormon material the minute they discovered I had recently joined the Church." When her former minister also gave her several books about how "terrible" the Mormons are, she told him, "I think it is interesting that the Mormons have never given me any books bashing other religions."

Like these recent converts, sooner or later most Latter-day Saint young people have to deal with anti-Mormon literature in one form or another. Just as the wicked witch in *The Wizard of Oz* appears to torment and frighten Dorothy, anti-Mormon literature also seems to appear in an attempt to pull us from the right path. How does Dorothy stay on track? She finds help in the form of three friends.

THINK IT THROUGH

Dorothy's first friend is a scarecrow who learns to use his brain. We can also think through what we read or hear about the Church that doesn't make sense. One teenager found it easy to recognize exaggerations ("Brigham Young had over 400 wives") and unsupported generalizations ("All Mormons are prejudiced"), but when he came across something he had never heard before, he went to his parents or seminary teacher for help. That was a smart choice.

Once a friend at school told him that Joseph Smith had recited many different versions of the First Vision and challenged, "If your prophet was telling the truth, why did he change his story through the years?"

The question bothered this young man throughout the day, but later when he shared it with his father, his dad wasn't bothered at all. He simply responded, "It's true there are various versions of Joseph's first vision which were prepared at different times for different audiences. How many versions have you heard of how your mother and I met?"

The teenager laughed as he said, "Well there is *your* version in which you were 'cautious' and then *Mom's* version in which you were 'scared.' There is the short version, the long version, and the spiritual version if you are telling it in a talk or lesson."

Then Dad said, "But in each telling the main elements—the truth of what happened—don't really change. Don't you think the same could be true for Joseph Smith?"

A young missionary was concerned when one of his investigators passed him material about connections between the Freemasons and the Mormons. He had never even heard of the Masons and was disturbed to read that Joseph Smith and many other early Church leaders belonged to this organization. The article claimed that the temple ceremony was "stolen" from Masonic rituals. He approached his mission president, who helped him think it through.

"The Masons are not a religion," explained his mission president, "although many members are religious. It is more like a fraternity or brotherhood—a service organization similar to the Boy Scouts." The mission president also explained that Joseph and other Church leaders were members, as were many of the Founding Fathers of the

United States, including George Washington. In frontier America the organization was much more popular than it is today.

"But what does that have to do with the temple?" asked the missionary.

"Masons claim to be one of the oldest organizations in the world, named in honor of the builders of Solomon's temple. They claim many of their symbols and traditions come from those ancient roots. Joseph Smith received the temple ordinances by revelation, and naturally they are also connected to ancient temples."

The missionary president continued to explain that it was similar to the sacrament or baptism. Many churches participate in similar ordinances, but they have been changed and altered through the years. Joseph did not present totally new and unrecognizable ordinances. Through revelation, the Prophet restored them to their pure and original form.

The mission president said, "I've always believed that the similarities between Mason and Mormon ceremonies actually stand as evidence that Joseph did not copy. Think about when a student copies a report and tries to change words so he will not be caught. If Joseph were copying or making the whole thing up, why didn't he simply change the elements that are the same? He couldn't. As a mouthpiece for God, he was not at liberty to change one speck of what was revealed to him."

TRUST YOUR FEELINGS

Dorothy's second friend is a tin man who learns to use his heart. We can also learn to trust our feelings, which are often influenced by the Holy Spirit (see 1 Nephi 17:45). A mother and her teenage son had recently joined the Church and were quite happy with their decision until their extended family began bombarding them with anti-Mormon literature. They stopped reading in the scriptures and attending Church. They refused to see members of the ward who tried to visit. Finally, the missionaries were able to speak with them. The mood in the home that had been so joyful just a few weeks before was now dark and gloomy.

For quite some time the mom and her son took turns firing accusations and questions at the missionaries, who tried their best to clarify Church principles and practices. Finally, one of the elders said, "This is really getting us nowhere. I think it would be much better if you simply search your feelings. When were you happiest and most united?"

The mother admitted, "When we were listening to the missionaries and attending Church."

"When were your minds clear and unconfused?"

The son said, "When we were reading the Book of Mormon and praying."

The missionary said, "Trust those feelings. There is nothing wrong with finding out more about the Church, but not in a way that makes you unhappy, angry, and closes you off from the world."

HAVE COURAGE

Dorothy's third friend is a lion who learns to have courage. We can do the same as we defend our beliefs and share our testimonies. We do not have to be experts in Church doctrine or history to have a testimony. Nephi said, "I know that [God] loveth his children; nevertheless, I do not know the meaning of all things" (1 Nephi 11:17).

Elder W. Grant Bangerter of the Seventy has written the following:

Although we should treat others with kindness, tolerance, and respect, we must stand firmly for the things that have been revealed to us. We do not apologize that we do not have the same doctrines and principles that other churches have. We can talk about it in a warm and friendly way, but we do not apologize. We didn't initiate this restoration. God did. If others do not appreciate the Church or its doctrines, we nevertheless know they are true.[14]

Following her baptism, a woman in Spain began to question her decision as a friend gave her anti-Mormon literature. The missionaries set an appointment to speak with her about her doubts, but she never showed up. They called her, but she didn't answer.

The following day they made contact, and she confessed she had been at her friend's house, where he was showing her more anti-Mormon literature. The missionary asked, "If this friend is the one causing your doubts, why were you there instead of with us who are trying to resolve those doubts?" His companion said, "If you want to find out more about the Church, ask us. Don't ask people who are not even members of it." They challenged her to read in the Book of Mormon and not put her Church attendance on hold as she sought answers to her questions.

Over the next few weeks, the woman showed great courage in keeping her commitments and also finally telling her friend she no longer wanted to read all the material he was supplying. She told him, "You seem very anxious to pull me away from what I have without offering anything better in its place."

To the missionaries, she said, "I don't understand why so many go out of their way to tear down the beliefs of others. Why don't they just promote their own beliefs? I still have questions—lots of questions. However, I know the Book of Mormon is true, and I can hold on to that for now."

Elder Davenport, who served his mission in Chile, spoke in a zone conference and said, "I have met members of other churches who are quick to tell me I am going to hell for not believing as they do. At first I was too timid to stand up to them. Then I started thinking about it. Here we are teaching that everyone will have the chance to hear the gospel and be baptized so they don't have to go to 'hell,' and here they are sending people there as fast as they can. I'm glad to be in the business of saving souls and not condemning them."

What do we do when they say it's not true? The Scarecrow, Tin Man, and Cowardly Lion help Dorothy face and overcome the wicked witch. As we use our brains, trust our feelings, and show courage, we too can stay on the path and reach our final destination.

WHAT I TRIED

All parents and leaders wonder about how much exposure to other religions and anti-Mormon thought is appropriate for young people who are still formulating their own testimonies. As with teaching "the facts of life," we don't want to overwhelm with too much information too soon. We also worry that by presenting information, we are somehow promoting or condoning. My experience has taught me that the opposite is true. The most vulnerable teens are usually the least informed. It is silence and ignorance, not open communication, that often leads to poor choices.

My wife, Debi, and I have tried to help our children understand that having doubts and asking questions are not wrong or a sign of weakness. Didn't Joseph Smith himself doubt and question as he learned? He said, "In the midst of this war of words and tumult of opinions, I often said to myself: What is to be done? Who of all these parties are right; or, are they all wrong together? If any one of them be right, which is it, and how shall I know it?" (Joseph Smith—History 1:10). The Church's missionary effort is an invitation to the world to escape tradition's chains and test present beliefs against revealed truth. Having doubts is not an evidence of wrongdoing; attempting to resolve doubt can be a step toward right. Asking questions is not a sign of weakness, but a sign of growth. We are not wrong when we doubt but only when we fail to do something about our doubts. "Prove all things," the scriptures say. But the learning process is not complete until the test is done, the experiments finished, and the conclusions drawn. "Prove all things" and "hold fast that which is good" (1 Thessalonians 5:21). Joseph Smith wrote, "and not understanding . . . , I inquired and received."[15]

Our family has tried to show respect for other religions. When members of other faiths knock at our door we tell them that, though we are not interested in listening to their message, we admire their dedication and devotion. We thank them for their time. When we pass street preachers who are screaming their protests outside a temple open house or general conference, we simply explain to the children that these misinformed people are fulfilling Moroni's prophecy that Joseph Smith's name would be known for good and evil among all nations (see Joseph Smith—History 1:33). We point out that Jesus faced the same kind of opposition in his day. When we speak of other faiths or religions, we try to do it in a positive tone, focusing on similarities as well as differences.

Perhaps the most direct efforts we have made have been to try to help our children understand that just because something is written in a book or found on the Internet doesn't make it correct. Whenever they bring up something they heard, we ask the qualifications of the one promoting the idea or the quality of the publication or TV program from which it came. Teaching children to evaluate the source of the information is an important step in helping young people learn to listen and think critically.

RUSSELL'S RESPONSE

In all honesty I can't remember a specific time in my life when my mom and dad told me it was okay to doubt. I must not have been home whenever missionaries of another faith knocked at our door, and I can't recall a time when I consciously tried to think critically about anti-Mormon teachings. I do, however, remember growing up in an environment where I felt safe to be open and honest. There was never a question or topic that was off limits to discussion. No parent can possibly prepare each child with an answer to every anti-Mormon argument, but parents can provide an environment for testimony growth.

A story from the Old Testament shows the importance of each individual strengthening his own testimony and not just relying on the testimony of others. It is the story of David and Goliath. When King Saul finally consented to let David fight Goliath, we are told that "Saul armed David with his armour, and he put an helmet of brass upon his head; also he armed him with a coat of mail" (1 Samuel 17:38). Overwhelmed by the size and weight of the unfamiliar armaments, "David said unto Saul, I cannot go with these; for I have not proved them. And David put them off him" (1 Samuel 17:39).

All young people lean on their parents' or church leaders' testimonies at one point or another. I know I did. All young people also arrive at the point when they need to take off their parents' armor and start proving their own. My first few days in the mission field were a real eye-opening experience. I did not expect everyone to be baptized because of my testimony, but for some reason I never expected anyone to ridicule or fight against it. As a missionary, I testified many times a day, and it was hard to see eyes roll, to be cut off midsentence, and to be laughed at as I shared my testimony with others.

My dad says he always tried to treat other religions with respect. That's true. For most of my life we've lived next door to a Baptist church. I remember one day when some neighborhood kids were standing out on the lawn and chanting, "Mormons are better than Baptists. Mormons are better than Baptists," as their church service was ending. My dad hurried over and quieted the children. I remember that he explained to them that they wouldn't want anyone doing the same thing to us as we finished church.

Growing up in a home where such respect was the norm, I was a little unprepared for the disrespect I encountered as a missionary. Maybe it would have been helpful to hear fewer happy-ending mission stories and a little more about the prejudice and rudeness I would encounter so I could have had a little thicker skin.

Still, David had never fought against a giant before he stood against Goliath. Would it have helped to have someone tell him it was going to be tough? Maybe not. David's best preparation were his previous experiences during which he had built trust in the Lord. That is what gave him the confidence to say to his foe, "Thou comest to me with a sword, and with a spear, and with a shield: but I come to thee in the name of the Lord of hosts" (1 Samuel 17:45). Did Goliath roll his eyes? Probably. Did he laugh? Of course. In fact, we could say he laughed his head off!

Before my mission, I, like David, had never had anyone challenge my testimony, but thanks to my parents' example and the things I had been taught in our home, I had learned to put my trust in the Lord. That allowed me not to give up when times got hard. Like David, I was able to find courage in the strength of the Lord and keep testifying regardless of ridicule.

KEYS FOR ACTION

What Can We Do FOR Young People?

We can remind young people they don't have to have all the answers. It is simple to explain that any question or concern usually hinges on whether or not Joseph Smith was a prophet. And we can know that by reading the Book of Mormon. Young people need to remember they are not alone. If someone is expressing a sincere desire to learn, they can involve the missionaries or other friends from the Church. Still, nothing is more awkward than being caught unprepared to answer a question about the Church—especially when it comes from someone in a group. We can help young people formulate a few simple responses to some of the most common questions and criticisms they will hear. For example:

Why didn't the blacks get the priesthood until 1978? Today all worthy males can hold the priesthood. There was a time when God denied that, just as he denied it to all but the descendents of Levi, one of the sons of Israel in the Old Testament, and just as he withheld the gospel from the Gentiles until after the death of Jesus in the New Testament. We don't know why, but perhaps we are too quick to assume it was for something the blacks did or did not do. Perhaps God had to wait until the minds and hearts of whites across the world were changed and softened so the work could move forward.

Why aren't women given the priesthood? Men and women are totally equal in the Church, but that does not mean they are the same. Women lead and participate in all levels of the Church. In fact, the Relief Society is the oldest and largest women's organization in the world. Worthy men have the priesthood, but they don't have a corner on the blessings of the priesthood. The saving ordinances and the blessings of membership are for everyone—male and female. Men and women need each other, and we believe that neither a man nor a woman can obtain the greatest possible blessings by him- or herself. They reach those goals together. We don't know why the Lord requires priesthood service of men, any more than we know why he has reserved childbearing for women.

What about polygamy? It is not practiced by Mormons today and anyone who lives in such a way is not a member of the Church, regardless of what he or she may claim. Still, there was a time when the practice was part of our history, and under prophetic direction, some men and women were called to live it, just as some Old Testament patriarchs were called to live it. The restoration of the gospel was a restoration of all things. When polygamy's purpose was completed, God revealed that it was no longer necessary.

What about intolerance against same-sex marriages? We believe that sexual relations are special and should be reserved only for marriage. We believe that men and women should not engage in sexual relations before or outside of their marriage to each other. We don't support same-sex marriage because we believe marriage is much more than a contract between two people. It is a divinely appointed institution, revealed to Adam and Eve. The emotional and physiological differences between men and women give deep meaning to the Lord's declaration: "Therefore shall a man leave his father and his mother, and shall cleave unto his wife: and they shall be one flesh" (Genesis 2:24). In that union (and only in that union) can another divine injunction be obeyed: "And I, God, created man in mine own image, in the image of mine Only Begotten created I him; male and female created I them. And I, God, blessed them, and said unto them: Be fruitful, and multiply, and replenish the earth" (Moses 2:27–28).

Are Mormons Christians? Of course we are. Some people who claim we are not Christians do so because we do not agree with some common Christian beliefs, but those beliefs did not originate with Christ. They were decided upon hundreds of years after his death. We are not third-century Christians, but we are most assuredly Christians. Any who wonder need only to consider the name of the Church and examine the lives of its members. As those who presume to judge us learn of our welfare system and humanitarian aid, they will see evidences that our faith is deeply rooted in Christian principles and a sincere belief in His injunction that we are to love and serve one another. The doctrines of The Church of Jesus Christ of Latter-day Saints are centered in the atonement and resurrection of Christ, who we testify is the Savior and Redeemer of the world.

What Can We Do WITH Young People?

It can be very informative to go with a nonmember friend to his or her worship services. We certainly like it when visitors come to our meetings. Not only can such visits spark discussion, but they can also help young people appreciate the Church they sometimes take for granted. Participating in an interfaith service project, holiday devotional, or choir festival can be very rewarding. We must be careful not to miss our own meetings and responsibilities in order to go, but with a little advanced planning, such interaction can break down misconceptions on all sides.

What Can Young People Do BY THEMSELVES?

It is more beneficial and certainly faith promoting to spend our time studying the gospel rather than reading anti-Mormon materials. Secure people don't worry too much about what others think of them. It is the insecure who are forever concerned about what "they" say. It is good to be informed, but not dominated, driven, or defined by others' opinions.

Part Three:

RESOURCES

▲ ▲ ▲

"An essential part of conversion is receiving a witness from
the Holy Ghost that the Book of Mormon is true. . . .
You have the great opportunity of working with many
leaders and members during your mission. . . . The relationships
you establish . . . will bless you for the rest of your life."

Preach My Gospel, *103, 213*

5

▲ ▲ ▲

OUR SICKLE:
THE BOOK OF MORMON

"What's a sickle?" That is the question elders and sister missionaries were asked by Elder D. Todd Christofferson of the Presidency of the Seventy. He had been assigned to reorganize a stake in Santiago and while there also consented to speak to the missionaries. During his talk, he referred to the fourth section of the Doctrine and Covenants where missionaries are instructed, "For behold the field is white already to harvest; and lo, he that thrusteth in his sickle with his might, the same layeth up in store that he perisheth not, but bringeth salvation to his soul" (v. 4).

The missionaries were slow to respond. Most had not come from farming backgrounds and were not sure what a sickle was. Even those who had grown up on farms were unfamiliar with this simple hand tool, which was commonly used before the development of the large machinery of today. Some had seen pictures of wheat being cut with an implement that had a curved blade and finally concluded that a sickle is a tool used to harvest grain.

Elder Christofferson verified the answer and then asked, "Now, what's *our* sickle? What tool are we using to harvest?"

One missionary raised his hand and responded with confidence: "Our sickle is the Book of Mormon."

Elder Christofferson agreed. He then bore testimony of the

power of that tool and the abundant harvest that awaits us when we use it effectively. A sickle is a unique tool that gathers, cuts, and harvests. The Book of Mormon does the same thing.

GATHERING

The long, curved blade on the sickle allows workers to efficiently cut a large swath of wheat in one swipe. In testifying of Jesus Christ, the Book of Mormon touches hearts and souls, gathering believers from every nation and culture. The title page of the Book of Mormon says it was written "to the convincing of the Jew and Gentile that Jesus is the Christ, the Eternal God, manifesting himself unto all nations."

One young woman said, "I recently joined the Church of Jesus Christ, but I had been blessed to grow up in a religious home. We learned lots of songs about Jesus and how he loves everyone. Still, even when I was little, I thought it was strange that if he loved everyone, he would come only to the people who lived in ancient Israel. I never said anything about it, but it was a thought that crossed my mind. Imagine my surprise when one day my friends asked, 'Did you know that Jesus Christ came to the Americas after his death and resurrection in the Holy Land?'"

Her Mormon friends showed her the scripture in John where Jesus says, "And other sheep I have, which are not of this fold: them also I must bring, and they shall hear my voice; and there shall be one fold, and one shepherd" (John 10:16).

The young woman said, "It was as if they had read my private childhood thoughts. I was thrilled to think that Jesus had gone to others besides the people in Jerusalem. I thought of those songs I had learned about how Jesus loved everyone. They really were true."

The Savior commanded his disciples, "Go ye into all the world" (Mark 16:15). Since when did Jesus ever expect from his disciples something he was unwilling to do himself? Just as he was baptized as an example, he also went into all the world as an example.

In 2 Nephi 29:8 we read, "Know ye not that the testimony of two nations is a witness unto you that I am God, that I remember one nation like unto another? Wherefore, I speak the same words unto one nation like unto another. And when the two nations shall run together the testimony of the two nations shall run together also."

CUTTING

A sickle is a sharp instrument that cuts the wheat. The Book of Mormon is also a sharp tool that cuts through years of apostasy, false perceptions of God and Christ, and mistranslations of the Bible. Elder Dallin H. Oaks has said, "Written by inspiration, [the Book of Mormon] is an unfailing antidote for the doctrinal confusion and behavioral excesses of our day."[16]

Not only does the book speak of Christ's visit to the Americas, but of prophets who wrote clearly of Christ's teachings, divinity, atonement, resurrection, and relationship to us. Their record reverberates with his name and spirit on every page. In fact, the Book of Mormon speaks about Christ on the average of every 1.7 verses. It mentions the Atonement more than any other scripture: thirty-six times, compared to only once in the New Testament, three times in the Pearl of Great Price, and eleven times in the Doctrine and Covenants.

When Grandma and Grandpa Wilcox were on their mission in Macon, Georgia, one of their assignments was to deliver copies of the Book of Mormon to those who requested them after viewing a televised Church commercial. One evening they found an address they had been given, approached the front door, and knocked.

A man answered and asked them who they were. Grandma said, "We are missionaries of the Church of Jesus Christ and are here to deliver the copy of the Book of Mormon you ordered." She showed him the book.

"Well," he said. "What is it?"

Grandma explained, "This is the Book of Mormon. It is another testament of Jesus Christ."

To which the man responded, "*Another* testament? Why *another* testament? Jesus has the Bible. That's testament enough."

Grandpa asked, "How many Christian churches are there?"

The man responded, "Maybe two or three hundred. Perhaps even as many as four hundred."

"In actuality," said Grandpa, "there are thousands—thousands of Christian denominations—all testifying of Christ in thousands of different ways, all interpreting the same Bible and doctrine in thousands of different ways. Maybe another testament of Christ is exactly what we need." The man accepted the book.

In Jesus' time there were faithful Jews who loved the Old Testament and expressed feelings similar to those of this man. When those Jews heard early New Testament Saints speak of their faith in Christ and new revelations, some probably feared such testimonies threatened to replace the Old Testament. However, believers learned it was not necessary to reject the old in order to believe the new. The two testaments complemented each other and were written to the same end—each testifying of Jesus Christ. Ultimately the two separate collections of sacred writings were brought together—literally bound together—so that many have come to think of them as one book.

In the same way, the Book of Mormon is not to displace the Bible but to be a second witness of the truths contained therein. It is interesting to note that having gone through only one (inspired) translation, the Book of Mormon in many, many instances teaches gospel principles more clearly than the Bible.

But there is another reason for the existence of the Book of

Mormon. Paul the Apostle restated an ancient standard of truth when he said: "In the mouth of two or three witnesses shall every word be established" (2 Corinthians 13:1). The Bible is one witness of Christ, and the Book of Mormon is another, both testifying that God is the same yesterday, today, and forever.

One missionary testified, "The Book of Mormon changes lives. It tells it like it is and that's what the world needs. It's not a politically correct book. It speaks the truth with clarity, and it is not afraid of offending those who need to be offended. I've seen people change their lives because of that book. It has changed mine."

Another enthusiastic missionary said, "The Book of Mormon has a voice and it is more powerful than ours. It can say things in a strong way. Our voices might reach someone's ears, but the Book of Mormon is the voice that cuts right to someone's core."

Yet another missionary felt the sharpness of this harvesting tool in his own life. He said, "In the world, time is divided between before and after Christ. My life can be divided into before I read the Book of Mormon and after I read it because that is when I became aware of Christ in my world."

HARVESTING

A sickle gathers and cuts, but not without purpose. Its purpose is to harvest. The Book of Mormon is not meant to be just another interesting or inspirational book. Its purpose is also to harvest. Like every missionary's purpose, the Book of Mormon's purpose is to "invite others to come unto Christ *by helping them receive the restored gospel.*"[17]

This purpose is accomplished not only by the inclusive nature of the book and the powerful and clear doctrine it contains, but also by how it came to be. In its ability to harvest, the origin of the book is as powerful as its content.

The Bible came to us through the sacrifice of many people over the centuries, but the Book of Mormon came to us from an angel. The Bible was translated by many scholars and saints using their experience, talents, and abilities. The Book of Mormon was translated by Joseph Smith, a young man with little formal education who had no experience, talent, or innate ability when it came to translating ancient texts. The book came to us, as we are told right on the title page, by "the gift and power of God." For that reason the book stands as convincing evidence that Joseph Smith was a prophet—an ordinary man through whom God did extraordinary things. There simply is no other satisfactory explanation for the book's existence.

Joseph Smith is not the only person in frontier America to claim visions. During his youth an exciting religious revolution was sweeping the country. Many claimed to have had visions and organized new churches. Why is it, then, that Joseph's claims are still heard throughout the world while most of the others have long since been ignored and forgotten? What did Joseph provide that no one else provided to substantiate his claims?

The Book of Mormon is a tangible evidence we can hold in our hands to support the intangible visions we did not witness. It contains 500 pages filled with complex literary structures and parallels to much that is known about the old world. There are three dating systems, 300 references to chronology, and 700 references to geography, which are all maintained with amazing consistency. Add to this the fact that Joseph was an uneducated farm boy and produced the manuscript in about 90 days, sometimes translating up to ten pages a day. It took 47 scholars four years to translate the King James Version of the Bible at a rate of about one page a day.

The book Joseph translated was not about some futuristic place or event. It is a record of the past. Some religious writers find it safe to muse about the Second Coming or heaven since no one can discredit their predictions. However, a book about the past is different. It opens itself to inspection—even scrutiny—and as many times as the

Book of Mormon has been under the magnifying glass, it has always held up.

Some readers feel uncomfortable as they find out how Joseph translated the ancient record. They read how he used interpreters called the Urim and Thummim as well as a seer stone. The mention of such objects in today's world raises eyebrows, to say the least.

I once spoke to a group of seminary students who had questions about the Urim and Thummim. They were skeptical and wanted to know what these interpreters looked like and how they functioned. I am admittedly no expert on the subject, but I explained how they have been described by those who viewed them—something like a special set of glasses through which Joseph could look that in some way allowed him to know what the translation should be.

Then I asked the students how many had seen a popular movie at the time called *National Treasure*. The film tells the story of several treasure seekers who discovered an invisible map on the back of the original copy of the Declaration of Independence of the United States of America. The treasure hunters were aided in their search by a set of glasses supposedly invented by Benjamin Franklin through which they could look and see a map no one else could see.

I asked the young people, "How is it that most people who watch that movie will buy into the idea that a pair of glasses exists that allow people to see an invisible map, yet when we talk about 'glasses' with which Joseph could translate, most people dismiss the idea as impossible?"

This fictional movie grossed millions and ignited the imagination of viewers who had never before considered that there might be a hidden map and a way to view it. For a few hours in a movie theater, people were willing to open their minds to the possibility of "What if?" Yet, when we speak of Joseph Smith, many people close their minds and will not even give his claims the time they would spend watching a movie. They refuse to suspend judgment long enough to even consider the chance that, in this case, fact could be more compelling than fiction.

The seminary students asked me about the seer stone. One young woman said, "On the Internet there was something that said that Joseph claimed he translated using a seer stone interchangeably with the interpreters." I explained that Joseph indeed used both. The seer stone was described by those who saw it as being a small stone, about the size of an egg. It was not black, but was dark in color. Apparently, as Joseph translated, words would appear on the stone in English—so clearly that Joseph could actually read them and even spell them for his scribes when there was a question.

The girl said, "A stone? The size of an egg? Dark in color? With writing that would appear on it? How are we supposed to get people to believe *that?*"

I asked her to please pull her cell phone out of her pocket and then said, "It looks like your cell phone is hard like a stone and about the size of an egg. It's dark in color and has words that appear on it that you can read. How are people ever going to believe that?"

Though many people wish for a more academic or reasonable explanation of the translation process, they don't realize that such an explanation would weaken rather than strengthen the book's impact. Consider the Dead Sea Scrolls. They were discovered by a shepherd boy in 1947. He saw no angel who led him to the place where the scrolls were buried. Rather, he stumbled upon the cave. The scrolls have been translated by some of the most knowledgeable and respected scholars of our time. In fact, professors at Brigham Young University have been enormously helpful in the translation and preservation of those ancient records. The story of the discovery and translation of the Dead Sea Scrolls is reasonable and acceptable. Unlike the Book of Mormon, the Dead Sea Scrolls have caused little controversy, but they have also had little impact. We don't mean to disrespect the amazing find or the fascinating contents of the scrolls.

Historically, it was a discovery of great significance. However, we have yet to meet or even hear about one person whose life was changed or who got baptized or went to the temple because they read the Dead Sea Scrolls.

Conversely, the Book of Mormon's existence cannot be separated from stories of angels, interpreters, seer stones, and even the appearance of God and Jesus. Were it just a book filled with the teachings of ancient prophets, it would be no more valuable to us than the Dead Sea Scrolls. The Book of Mormon is evidence that there are prophets in our day, that God continues to reveal himself to man. That truly sets it apart.

The influence of both the Book of Mormon's teachings and its origin are explained in a wonderful book by Terryl L. Givens, *By the Hand of Mormon: The American Scripture That Launched a New World Religion.*[18] In that book the author also discusses the importance of the witnesses of the Book of Mormon. Before reading that book, I had never considered why the testimony of the three and eight are separated. Why is there not one statement signed by all eleven? Givens points out that the three witnesses did not see only the plates but also an angel, and they even heard the voice of God, declaring the truthfulness of the book. The testimony of the eight "is lacking in any traces of supernaturalism. Joseph Smith simply showed them the plates, allowing them to make their own examination and draw their own conclusions."[19] They saw the plates, handled them, described them, and even "hefted" them.

Givens writes, "Taken together, the two experiences seemed calculated to provide an evidentiary spectrum, satisfying a range of criteria for belief. The reality of the plates was now confirmed by both proclamation from heaven and by empirical observation, through a supernatural vision and by simple, tactile experience."[20] Those who would choose to disregard the supernatural as unbelievable cannot disregard the empirical observation, and the acceptance of one witness leads us to examine the other with increased interest.

In 2 Corinthians 13:1 we read, "In the mouth of two or three witnesses shall every word be established." Not only does this speak of the need for both the Bible and the Book of Mormon, it also speaks of the need for various witnesses of the Book of Mormon. The first witness is found in the combined testimony of three. The second witness is found in the combined testimony of eight. Add to them a third, that of Joseph Smith himself, and we have twelve—a quorum of twelve—establishing the word.

The introduction to the Book of Mormon makes it clear that as we come to know its truthfulness by the power of the Holy Ghost, we can also come to know that Joseph Smith is a prophet and that Jesus lives and has restored the fullness of his gospel in preparation for his second coming.

Such remarkable news can be accepted or rejected, but either way, it demands that we take sides. The Book of Mormon cannot be apathetically brushed aside like the Dead Sea Scrolls. Because of how the book came to be, we cannot ignore its teachings without facing serious consequences. The book is a call to action, a call to change. Those who pay little attention to the Book of Mormon are not just missing an interesting bit of history. They are literally missing salvation.

AN EFFECTIVE TOOL

The Book of Mormon is an effective tool in the work of bringing souls to Christ and giving them the power to make positive changes. It is amazing to see the impact it has and the difference it makes in the lives of those who are willing to read, ponder, and pray.

One missionary confessed, "I completed reading the Book of Mormon again yesterday. Independent of anything said by others— whether prophets or anti-Mormon street preachers—I have read the book for myself, and have my own testimony of it. I can say that I have learned more from that book than any other. I have become a better person as a result of reading it."

One convert, still dripping wet from his baptism, testified, "The Book of Mormon is proof that Jesus was resurrected and lives. Not just because he showed himself in the Americas. Not just because he showed himself to Joseph Smith, but because now he is alive for me. Jesus was dead in my life, but the Book of Mormon brought him to life for me."

Two elders were knocking on doors, and a man told them he wasn't interested so they moved on. Several minutes later, the same man caught up to them, carrying a copy of the Book of Mormon in his hand. He said, "When I moved into my house I found this book as I was cleaning. Would you tell me what it is?" The missionaries were happy to do so, and soon the man was progressing toward baptism. The missionaries were grateful for the member or missionary who placed that book with someone in that house, never suspecting that the one who was ready to receive it would be the next home owner.

Another set of missionaries taught a man and offered to give him a copy of the Book of Mormon. The man thought the title sounded familiar, so he hurried to his shelf and retrieved a copy someone had given him thirty years before. When he later joined the Church, he said, "For thirty years I had this book in my home, but now I have it in my heart. I am sad to think I could have had the truth thirty years ago if I had just opened the book that was already sitting on my shelf."

A sickle can be a useful and effective tool, but it does little good hanging unused in the toolshed. Even in the field it will not be productive for those who choose to wave it aimlessly in the air or casually brush it across the top of the wheat. Even the greatest of harvesting tools requires the thrust of a worker who knows how to use the tool and does so with all his might. Only then does "the same layeth up in store that he perisheth not, but bringeth salvation to his soul" (D&C 4:4).

WHAT I TRIED

There is so much confusion in the world about Jesus Christ. Some say he never existed at all. Others claim he was a prophet and a great teacher, but they don't think he was the son of God. Even many religious leaders doubt his divinity. On the other hand, some claim that he was a God who came to earth but never experienced mortal life as we know it.

Once I saw an article in a magazine that claimed to "expose the real Jesus" by saying that the words and teachings we attribute to him really came from his disciples at best and at worst were all made up by some monks in the Middle Ages. The article claimed that Christ never performed miracles. He didn't walk on water. He *waded* in it. He didn't heal the lame, but simply ministered to them and helped them feel better about themselves. It is not uncommon to hear the events of Christ's life as recorded in the Bible explained away by some as being nothing more than folktales—legends or fantastical stories passed down through the ages that became more exaggerated with every telling.

Such are the perspectives and beliefs that confront our children on all sides. That is why is it is so vital that our children come to know that the Book of Mormon provides a true perception of Jesus. Many LDS children love the stories of the Book of Mormon, and Debi and I shared them with our children, too. It is important that they know the characters and events. However, we also tried to point out the purpose of those stories is to teach us about the character and attributes of Christ—who he was, what he did, and the role he plays in our lives today. We wanted our children to know the stories, but more importantly, we wanted them to find Christ through the Book of Mormon.

Susan Easton Black wrote, "Unfortunately, many readers settle for something far less than finding Christ in the Book of Mormon. Failing to find the key, they fail to recognize the reason that has moved missionaries, pioneers, and Latter-day Saints to devote all to the quest. These Saints have discovered that the Book of Mormon is an amazingly rich and powerful witness of Jesus Christ."[21]

How do we know Jesus actually gave the Sermon on the Mount and that it was not made up by some monk in the Middle Ages? Because Jesus gave the same sermon almost word for word in the Americas. How do we know Jesus was actually divine and that he performed miracles and wasn't just a "really nice guy"? Because the Book of Mormon testifies, "The time cometh, and is not far distant, that with power, the Lord Omnipotent who reigneth, who was, and is from all eternity to all eternity, shall come down from heaven among the children of men, and shall dwell in a tabernacle of clay, and shall go forth amongst men, working mighty miracles. . . . And he shall be called Jesus Christ, the Son of God" (Mosiah 3: 5, 8).

While we served our mission in Chile, my youngest children, Whitney and David, attended an international school in Santiago. We appreciated the wonderful teachers and the multicultural environment. However, Whitney and David quickly realized that many of the teachers and students thought differently than they did. Our kids had to learn to defend their positions on everything from alcohol and drugs to gay marriage.

One day Whitney's teacher made the comment that he did not believe in God or Jesus. The teacher said, "There is no proof that either God or Jesus exist." Many in the class probably felt differently, but none voiced their opinions—except Whitney, who raised her hand and said, "But there *is* proof."

The teacher said, "Really? Proof besides your own belief?"

Whitney said, "Yes, it's called the Book of Mormon."

Of course, the teacher brushed her words aside. Not being familiar with the book's teachings or origin, he was unable to understand Whitney's comment. But the important thing is that Whitney understood. She recognized that the Book of Mormon is indeed tangible evidence that God and Jesus live, love us, and lead us today.

RUSSELL'S RESPONSE

I am proud of my younger sister and brother who learned to stand up for themselves against opposition. I don't think I would have had the courage to do that at their ages. It took me a lot longer to arrive where they are in their testimonies.

I don't think I fully appreciated what the Book of Mormon is and what it can do until right before my mission. I had the opportunity to be in Chile for a few weeks before I entered the MTC on my way to Málaga. While I was there, Elder Jeffrey R. Holland spoke to all the missionaries. I was excited for the opportunity to participate in the conference even though I was not yet a full-time missionary. I took careful notes as Elder Holland taught about how God's work must be done in God's way. I listened intently as Elder Holland focused on the power of the Book of Mormon in the conversion process. In the middle of his talk he stopped, looked down from the pulpit directly at me, and said, "Russell, you take the Book of Mormon to the people of Málaga." He then went right on with his talk without missing a beat. I replayed his words many times in my mind.

When I arrived in Spain, I realized why he emphasized the Book of Mormon. Without exception those investigators who progressed toward baptism were those who read the Book of Mormon. Not once did I see an investigator get baptized who had not had a spiritual experience with the Book of Mormon beforehand.

When my companion and I moved into a new apartment, our landlady, Adela, welcomed us warmly. She was eighty years old, had white hair, and though she was not a member of the Church, she had a copy of the Book of Mormon. A few years earlier some missionaries had given her a copy but never explained to her what it was or why it was important. As we began to teach Adela more about the importance of the book, she got really excited about reading it. When we came home for lunch we'd find her reading the book, and at night we'd hear her turning pages. She took notes and asked us lots of questions when we'd teach her. As her testimony grew, she decided to get baptized.

Adela joined the Church in November of 2005—the same year that President Hinckley had issued his challenge to the Saints to read the Book of Mormon before the end of the year. After Adela's baptism we told her of the prophet's direction and the promises that awaited those who followed through. During the Christmas holidays, she went to her daughter's house to spend the vacation with family. However, she hadn't quite finished reading the Book of Mormon. On New Year's Eve she asked her daughter to take her home early so she could finish the book before the end of the year as the prophet instructed. The next day she grabbed my shoulders with both arms and said, "Thank you for coming into my life and for bringing this book to me."

While working in the area of Fuengirola, we had a car and always kept a few extra copies of the Book of Mormon in the back seat. One day a young man about our age saw the Book of Mormon through the back window as he walked by and asked us if he could have a copy. We eagerly obliged and marked a few chapters for him to read. We learned his name was Shoucri and wrote down his phone number to see if he had questions later on. A few days later we called Shoucri and not only had he read the chapters we'd marked, but he had also started reading straight through from the beginning. He told us that he'd had a dream similar to Lehi's a few years earlier, but hadn't understood it until then. Shoucri continued reading in the Book of Mormon because he said doing so made him happy.

After attending church for several weeks, he asked me about "this baptism thing" he kept reading about. His question made me feel like a batter in a game of baseball who had just been thrown a very slow pitch. My companion and I taught him about baptism and just as we were getting ready to commit him to a date he asked, "So, when can I be baptized?" I felt like I was living inside a *New Era* article. On the day of Shoucri's baptism, he gave away over twenty copies of the Book of Mormon with his testimony written inside it to nonmember friends he'd invited to the ordinance.

When *Preach My Gospel* came out during the first months of my mission, I wasn't at all surprised to read, "The Book of Mormon, combined with the Spirit, is your most powerful resource in conversion."[22]

I grew up hearing Book of Mormon stories, quoting verses, and reading in the Book of Mormon. Even so, it wasn't until my mission that I was able to internalize the powerful message of the book and witness for myself its impact in changing lives. In following Elder Holland's direction to "take the Book of Mormon to the people of Málaga," I was able to fully appreciate the unique sickle God has provided us to use in the work of saving his children.

KEYS TO ACTION

What Can We Do FOR Young People?

Perhaps one of the greatest things we can teach young people is that when it comes to a testimony of truth they don't have to take our word for it. They can know for themselves. The Book of Mormon itself contains this assurance: "And if [these] are not the words of Christ, judge ye—for Christ will show unto you, with power and great glory, that they are his words" (2 Nephi 33:11).

Moroni's promise is not just good news for investigators. It is good news also for young Latter-day Saints who have grown up memorizing the Articles of Faith and attending church and seminary but who still need to know for themselves. The assurance that "by the power of the Holy Ghost ye may know the truth of all things" (Moroni 10:5) is a promise to member and nonmember, adult and teenager, teacher and student. The God who inspired Moroni to write that promise is the same God who later sent Moroni to Joseph Smith, and he is the same God who will fulfill the promise in the lives of those who seek with real intent.

What Can We Do WITH Young People?

It is not easy for some young people to share a copy of the Book of Mormon with their friends, but the experience can be extremely beneficial for the recipient as well as satisfying for the giver. They just need some coaching on how to do it effectively. We know of one elementary school girl who gave her teacher a Book of Mormon as a Christmas gift. When she handed him the present she said, "I'm sorry if you don't like it, but my mom made me give it to you." Interestingly enough, the teacher did like it, later joined the Church, and has thanked his former student and her family many times for their gift. Still, let's try to do a little better than "My mom made me give it to you."

A similarly ineffective approach is to put the book on a doorstep, ring the doorbell, and run away. We get a lot further with a person if in delivering the book we tell him why we appreciate or admire him, explain what the Book of Mormon is, and then share our own feelings—our testimony—of the book.

Consider the young man who invited his nonmember friend to a youth conference. The visitor enjoyed the dances, activities, and workshops. As the conference was coming to an end, the member thanked his friend for coming. He said, "We have been friends for a long time, but I don't think I have ever actually thanked you for being such a great friend. You know I am a Mormon, but maybe you don't know why people call us that. It's because of the Book of Mormon. It is the record of God's dealings with the ancient people of the Americas just as the Bible is the record of God's dealings with the people in the eastern hemisphere. The Book of Mormon tells about when Jesus visited the Americas."

The boy didn't go into an overview of the whole book. He didn't mention the names of any of the prophets, which his friend wouldn't have recognized. He just explained that it was a book, similar to the Bible, that talked about Jesus. That is all it takes.

Finally, the boy told his friend, "I may not be the best example for you all the time, but I want you to know that my life is better when I read this book and apply what I read. I am happier when I try to live by its teachings. That feeling assures me that the Book of Mormon is true, and that's why I want to share a copy with you."

What Can Young People Do BY THEMSELVES?

Elder David A. Bednar of the Quorum of the Twelve Apostles spoke to young people in a Church Educational System fireside on February 4, 2007, in which he told the young people that the scriptures are their key to accessing living water. He told them that along with reading the scriptures straight through to become familiar with them, they also need to explore and apply the scriptures. He suggested studying by topic and also by looking for patterns and connections.[23]

One young man who had recently received his mission call and had gone through the temple took Elder Bednar's advice. He said that until he started looking for themes in his reading, he never realized how many scriptures there were just on the first four principles of the gospel. He used the Topical Guide and also the footnotes. He began to see for himself how the Bible and the Book of Mormon go hand in hand. He also noticed similarities between how Nephi obtained the brass plates and how we gain our own testimonies. He saw fascinating connections between the temple endowment and King Benjamin's address. He noticed patterns in the way the various missionaries in the Book of Mormon taught the people. He became excited at the possibility of following these same patterns in his own mission. Along with examining the missionaries, he also found similarities among converts. He saw similarities in how Alma was born again and how King Lamoni came to a knowledge of the truth.

He said, "The words are the same words that have always been there, but now I see things I have never seen before. It's like the Liahona that had 'new writing, which was plain to be read, which did give us understanding concerning the ways of the Lord; and it was written and changed from time to time, according to the faith and diligence which we gave unto it'" (1 Nephi 16:29).

6

▲ ▲ ▲

IT'S ALL ABOUT WHO
YOU KNOW

"It's sure nice to know the right people," we say when someone lands a well-paying job. "He's got connections," we say when someone is given a part in the play or a position on the team. "It's all about who you know," we say when someone receives an award or recognition.

No one enjoys feeling as though the only reason he got a job was because of who his parents are or because strings were pulled. We have known friends who have even gone to great lengths *not* to use an inside contact or reveal a relationship that would have helped them along.

Whether or not who you know helps in the world of business, sports, or politics, one thing is sure: When it comes to the world of missionary work, it truly is all about who you know. Effective missionaries know their companions, investigators, and the members of the wards and branches in which they serve. They take time to get to know their ward mission leaders, bishops, and branch presidents. Most of all, they know the prophets, the Savior, and their Heavenly Father. With a team like that on our side, we are surrounded by some pretty high-powered and important friends who can help us out when times are hard. They may not pull strings for us, but they'll be pulling for us. They may not give us a handout, but they will always give us a hand. Some of the greatest resources missionaries have are those with whom they labor. When we are engaged in the Lord's work, we are never alone.

COMPANIONS

A newly called missionary was nervous as the time drew closer for him to enter the MTC. He said, "I'm just so scared about who my companion will be. What if he is a jerk, geek, or loser? What if he is a computer nerd or a punk?"

His older brother said, "Whoever it is, you'd better get past all your stereotypes and labels pretty fast. You are going to have to work with that elder 24/7 and the only way you can do that is to get to know him and appreciate him for who he is."

One missionary discovered this: "In high school there are always groups, but in the mission you lose that. Everyone is just a person. You learn to look beyond the labels."

Looking back at our missions, we are thankful for the companions who put up with us and showed patience and support as we grew. Our lives have been greatly enriched by the friendships made with companions and fellow missionaries.

Still, living with a companion can present some of the greatest challenges of the mission. Two people come together from totally different backgrounds and families, and yet they have to learn to put aside their differences and work in unity and love. Where the missionaries fail to do that, for whatever reason, the work suffers. On the other hand, companionships where the two are patient, kind, respectful, and loving of each other almost always find people to teach and baptize.

INVESTIGATORS

I once heard Elder Francisco J. Viñas of the First Quorum of the Seventy tell a group of missionaries, "If you are going to call yourself a shepherd, you'd better smell like the sheep." We may have a great message to share with wonderful scriptures and examples, but we won't get the chance to use them unless we are out among the people and they sense our genuine care and concern.

Since returning home, Russell has stayed in contact with some of his converts. One mother has continued to attend church with her children, but privately she writes to him, "It's just not the same since you left."

"Why?" asks Russell. "Don't the missionaries come by?"

"Yes," she responded. "In fact, they come for lunch regularly, and they even share a thought or scripture before they leave. But they don't care about me."

Russell and his companion didn't spend undue amounts of time at her home or focus exclusively on her at church meetings, but when they saw her they always asked how she was and listened when she responded. They knew her name and family situation. They expressed their concern for her well-being. That personal interest was what she was missing.

A returned sister missionary who served in Australia wrote to a woman she had helped bring into the Church. The woman never responded. Finally, after many months, the returned missionary wrote, "Look, I know something is wrong or you would have written long ago. You just need to know that I don't care what it is. If you have stopped going to church or if you have slipped up in living the Word of Wisdom, or whatever it is, I still love you. I will always love you no matter what."

Not long after, she received a phone call from the woman. Sure enough, she had been struggling to stay active, but she felt the love of this sister missionary and it gave her new hope. As they spoke to each other, the woman committed to read the Book of Mormon all the way through and resume attending church, even though her nonmember husband made it difficult for her to do so.

There is a bond that grows between missionaries and their

converts because they have learned to care so deeply about each other. Whether it is Russell in Spain or this sister missionary in Australia, missionaries need to know and love their investigators and converts. Take time to ask about how things are going at work or school. Find out about their parents or children. Write a note or call to assure your investigators that you will be waiting for them at the chapel. Bake some banana bread and drop it off so they know you are thinking of them. There are those who warn that such efforts convert people to the missionary and not to the gospel. But how will the people ever be converted to the gospel if they don't see it being lived?

WARD MEMBERS

"The members never help us!" Although that is a common complaint for missionaries, they need to ask themselves how much they helped the missionaries prior to their own missions. We can all do better. Just remember that reprimands and guilt trips administered over the pulpit are usually not as effective in motivating members as is getting to know them. A sign on the wall of a doctor's office reads: "The first step to helping your patients is knowing your patients." Learn names. Find out how long people have been members or lived in the ward. Invite ward members to help with specific tasks and thank them when they do.

One woman scrimped all week long to be able to buy chicken to serve the missionaries on her assigned day. Her own children went without the night before so she could provide a nice meal for the elders. Imagine her disappointment when instead of receiving a sincere thank you, one missionary looked at his companion and said, "Chicken and rice again? That's the fifth time this week!"

Members need to be treated with the same respect and tact we hope they will show as they interact with investigators. Christopher B. Munday, who served as the president of the England Birmingham

Mission, always told his missionaries to avoid working with the same willing members time and time again. He encouraged his missionaries to ask, "Who needs to work with us?" rather than just, "Who will work with us?" By reaching out to everyone in the ward, the elders and sisters were able to increase the number of referrals they received and improve their overall effectiveness.

Two sister missionaries finished their dinner appointment by asking for references as they always did. The grandma-aged woman who had provided the meal said, "The only time I leave is to shop or go to church. I'm sorry, but I don't have any references for you."

One of the sisters said, "Then will you help us in another very important way? I am going to write a list of our progressing investigators. Will you please pray for them every day by name?" The woman agreed and followed through. She was thrilled to be able to help the missionaries in her own way.

There is no doubt that the most effective teaching takes place when the full-time missionaries are accompanied by members. Everyone agrees on that, and the results speak for themselves. The problem is that sometimes it is difficult for members to fit "one more thing" into their schedules—especially at the last minute. If the missionaries want members to be involved, they have to make the effort to plan ahead.

When a new elder moved into a ward, he paid special attention to the youth. He learned the names of the young people and went out of his way to greet and welcome the young men when they arrived at church. His senior companion teased him and said, "You're wasting your time. They are not investigators."

The younger elder said, "They are in a way. Many of them are still gaining their testimonies, so they need our support and encouragement, too. Maybe our examples will help them choose to serve missions."

In the weeks that followed, the senior companion noticed it was easier to find young men who were willing to accompany them on divisions and as a result they began getting more done. It turned out they did not have to wait till these young men received their own mission calls to see benefits from their efforts to befriend the youth.

One woman washed the clothes of the missionaries every week. When the elders suggested they could lighten her load by looking for others to help or by doing it themselves, she responded, "Please don't deny me the blessings of helping. I cannot do a lot of things, but I can wash clothes. One day I want to wash the clothes of my Savior, but until then I will wash the clothes of the missionaries." That kind of attitude and service needs to be humbly appreciated.

WARD LEADERS

Missionaries are usually told that the first people they should visit when they arrive in their assigned ward or branch are the mission leader and the bishop or branch president. Obediently, most say hi, but only a few are wise enough to go the extra mile and truly get to know these key leaders, become friends, and sincerely offer to help lighten their loads.

Shortly after Russell arrived in Málaga, the stake was split and a new stake president was called. Even though Russell was new and still felt insecure about his ability to speak Spanish, he made it a point to seek out and congratulate the man after the meeting. That was the beginning of a friendship between the two of them. Whenever they crossed paths, Russell complimented him on something that was going well in the stake. Later, Russell and his companion invited the stake president to a zone conference where he spoke to the missionaries. The stake president then invited Russell and his companion to his home at Christmas time for a meal, and the missionaries presented the family with a simple gift. How could this stake president speak negatively about the missionaries when he knew them personally? How could he fail to respond if the missionaries had a need or concern?

In the same way, Russell always noticed it was easier to work with bishops when he took time to foster a friendship. These bishops would ask members to fast for the missionary work, attend baptismal services, and promptly give callings to new converts. Other bishops sometimes treated the missionaries like an additional burden or even as rivals who were somehow working against them. Not surprisingly, there was always more success and a better feeling in wards where missionaries and leaders were working together.

While serving as mission president in Chile, I tried to make sure the local priesthood leaders felt appreciated. Many were accustomed to hearing from a mission president only if there was a problem, so they were a little shocked when I would show up with a box of doughnuts or a small gift book just to say thanks for all they were doing. Rather than scheduling another meeting, the members of my mission presidency and I would take ward and stake leaders with us to visit less-active members, investigators, and recent converts. Anything the leaders needed to talk about in a meeting could usually be discussed as we traveled from house to house.

JOSEPH SMITH AND THE PROPHETS

When I was serving my first mission in Chile, my companion and I were teaching members of a family who were all progressing nicely except for the mother. She would greet us at the door with a long face and try to think of reasons not to let us come in. How many times can someone in the same house be contagious with a different life-threatening disease?

Her husband would invite her to listen to our lessons. Her children would invite her. Finally, she agreed to sit in, but only as long as the missionaries didn't say anything about Joseph Smith. She said,

"The elders can talk about Jesus all they want and I will listen, but if they start talking about Joseph Smith, I'm leaving."

It was her twelve-year-old son who explained, "Mom, you just don't get it. To know Jesus, you have to know Joseph." He was right. It is only as we come to know the Prophet Joseph, his revelations, his teachings, and the scriptures he translated that we see the Savior for who he is.

More recently, I had a missionary in the mission who was greatly concerned about the focus being placed on Joseph Smith during the 200th anniversary of the birth of the Prophet. He felt there were too many songs, programs, firesides, and talks giving "Praise to the Man." In an interview, the elder expressed his frustration, saying, "Look, I admire all Joseph Smith went through as much as the next guy, but it is Jesus who is our Savior. It was Jesus who restored his Church through the Prophet. It was not Joseph who restored the Church. Shouldn't we be focusing all this attention on Jesus?"

His points were valid. Given the emotions associated with the celebration, perhaps members and missionaries were not being as sensitive as they should have been. Still, I explained to the elder, "Just as Jesus provides a window to his Father, Joseph provides a window to the Savior. In honoring one, we honor all."

A sister missionary wrote in a weekly letter to the president, "I really am enjoying learning so much about Joseph Smith. I think my tendency at the beginning of my mission was to downplay Joseph since I didn't want anyone to mistakenly think we worship a man. But now I know that Joseph Smith is way too important to downplay. It is only as we come to know Joseph and the authorized prophets and apostles who have followed him that we see a complete vision of this work."

Some have had the honor of meeting prophets personally, but one does not need to meet them to know them. We can read their words, listen to their counsel, learn of their lives, and apply their teachings.

I will never forget arriving at the Salt Lake City International Airport and noticing the place was in quite an uproar. Everyone was excitedly looking and pointing. I asked a worker close by what was happening, and the worker said that a famous country singer had just arrived and was walking through the airport. It seemed everyone knew the country singer and was straining to get a peek at the celebrity.

I made my way out of the terminal, and just as I was leaving, I noticed Elder Russell M. Nelson of the Quorum of the Twelve Apostles entering the building with members of his family. I don't often get the opportunity to see the Brethren up close, so as Elder Nelson approached, I stepped aside to watch him pass. When Elder Nelson made eye contact, I said, "God bless you, Elder Nelson, for the good you do."

Elder Nelson nodded and simply said, "Thanks." Just then several businessmen also walked by, laughing and swearing, and I thought, *They have no idea who they just passed. They just walked by an apostle of the Lord Jesus Christ and they have no clue!*

How ironic it is that a famous country singer can arrive in Salt Lake and create such a stir, while an apostle can walk through the same airport and go unnoticed by many. Paul instructed the Saints of his time to "know them which labour among you, and are over you in the Lord" and admonished them further "to esteem them very highly in love for their work's sake" (1 Thessalonians 5:12–13). We would do well to heed that counsel today.

JESUS CHRIST AND HEAVENLY FATHER

After serving for a while, a missionary in Chile said, "Knowing God and Jesus is what makes everything fit together. If you don't understand their natures, their relationship with us, and their plan for us, then you never understand their dealings with us." His words were very similar to what Joseph Smith taught in *Lectures on Faith*, which was that true faith is more than just knowing there is a God. It is knowing God and living according to His plan for us.

A young man once gave a seminary devotional in which he held up a poster of an adorable puppy with a caption that said, "To Know Him Is to Love Him." The picture was met with sighs from all the girls in the class. The young man then replaced the picture with a portrait of the Savior, and underneath he left the same caption: To Know Him Is to Love Him. He explained that our love for the Savior and our Father in Heaven deepens as we come to know them better through study, prayer, and feeling the Spirit's influence in our lives.

The young man was correct, but there is an additional way to know them better and that is through service. King Benjamin taught, "For how knoweth a man the master whom he has not served, and who is a stranger unto him, and is far from the thoughts and intents of his heart?" (Mosiah 5:13).

As missionaries fill their minds with thoughts of the Savior and their hearts with love and gratitude for the Savior, they will naturally fill their days with acts of the Savior. Painting a school, replacing windows at an orphanage, reading to disabled children, pulling weeds from a garden, helping a family move—these are all part of missionary work because it's all part of serving others.

Of course, there are limits to the services missionaries provide. Two elders were knocking on doors in Santiago, and the senior companion was explaining to his brand-new greenie that offering service can be an effective way to get into some houses. A few doors later, a woman called from an open window, "Not now, I'm showering." The new missionary didn't understand her Spanish and thought she said she was washing clothes. You can imagine everyone's shock when he called back, "May we help you?"

Sister Wilcox and I attended a lot of meetings during our

mission, but one of our favorites was always the final testimony meeting before the elders and sisters left for home. The missionaries were asked to begin by sharing an episode in Christ's life. Many shared scripture stories that had become more meaningful during their missions, but it was always apparent that the stories they most wanted to share were not just those found in scriptures. They weren't content to simply talk about the miracles of long ago. They wanted to talk about miracles they had witnessed right now in their sectors. They weren't content to talk about Christ's influence in the past. They wanted to talk about the lives he is changing today.

For too many, Christ is nothing more than an eternal baby in a manger or a perpetual suffering figure upon a cross. For missionaries, he is alive and guiding their steps. They love the "good news" shared by Matthew, Mark, Luke, and John, but they have their own good news to share as they have come to know Jesus and Heavenly Father by serving them.

WHAT I TRIED

Teamwork is an essential part of missionary success. Missionaries begin their missions thinking they will be a part of every step of the conversion process. Soon they discover that they are teaching people someone else found, and other missionaries are baptizing people they taught. They learn quickly that they cannot do it alone, but also that it's not even desirable to do so. President Gordon B. Hinckley said, "The progress of this work will be determined by our joint efforts."[24]

Just as on a sports team, nothing can destroy unity faster in missionary work than mistrust, competition, and jealousy. While such feelings shouldn't exist on a mission, they often creep in and cause problems. We start to mistrust fellow missionaries when they don't show up for an appointment. We feel a silent competition as other companionships are reporting higher numbers or more baptisms.

We feel jealous when other missionaries are given special assignments or called to leadership positions.

Just as members of a sports team need to do, missionaries must remember their joint purpose. Each must ask himself: *Did I come on a mission to build the kingdom or to build my own ego? Did I come because of the name I have taken upon myself or to make a name for myself?* If we truly have an eye single to God's glory, we will remember we are a team. The success or failure of each member reflects on the entire group.

I tried to teach this concept to Russell as he participated in various sports, but I'm not much of an athlete, so I don't know if that was the best context for me personally. I think it was more natural for me to teach teamwork within the context of family chores and projects, school activities, and Church responsibilities.

For example, when Russell would feel jealous of his sister because he felt she was getting an opportunity he wasn't, or when he felt like younger siblings were "getting off easy" when it came to chores, I would always remind him, "What's our goal here?" By keeping Russell focused on a larger purpose, he was able to see that everything didn't have to revolve around what he wanted in the moment.

When Russell ran for a student government office in his high school and lost the election by only a few votes, it was a hard experience. After the hurt of the moment passed, I reminded him that if his goal was to just get a title behind his name so he could feel important, then he had not reached it. However, if his goal was to help make the school a better place, there were lots of ways to accomplish that goal without holding an elected office.

RUSSELL'S RESPONSE

When my dad says he isn't much of an athlete, he is not kidding. My mom taught me most of what I know about sports. Still, my dad was always supportive when I played. He came to my games and always cheered for me.

I remember once when some friends and I wanted to play in a basketball league, but we couldn't enter the competition without a coach. None of the other dads would do it, so I turned in my dad's name. He was a little shocked when he found out about it and said, "But, Russell, I don't know the first thing about how to play!"

I replied, "Don't worry. We'll take care of everything. All you have to do is show up."

My plan worked out well until we had a really hard game and were getting creamed. All the team members looked to my dad for advice, and he just smiled and said, "Keep up the good work!"

I felt bad about having put him in that position, but my dad made the best of if. He was serving as the bishop of a BYU ward at the time, and he actually called one of the ward members, a young man who had been on a championship basketball team in California, and asked if he would be willing to help out.

With this new "assistant coach" on board, we really started to improve. We didn't win first place or anything, but we didn't have to run and hide either. Did I learn teamwork from that? I think I learned more about creative problem solving!

Looking back, I actually learned more about teamwork from watching my dad interact with other speakers and teachers at Especially for Youth or Campus Education Week—some of the teams on which he plays. There have been a few who have felt as though they were in competition with my dad through the years, and they would make comments such as, "Oh, no. I don't want to teach at the same time as you. No one will come to my class." I've seen how my dad tries to laugh off their comments and build up and encourage the other teachers.

I've also seen how he handles it when people make comments comparing Dad to other speakers or teachers. Dad always takes it in stride and says, "I'm glad you like what they are teaching you. They teach me a lot, too."

In private I once asked him, "Dad, doesn't it bug you to be compared all the time?" He said, "I just remember that we're all on the same team. We are fighting for the same purpose. We are all trying to accomplish the same goal, so their success is my success." And he really feels like that. These people are among his dearest friends and role models. He sincerely admires their many talents and abilities. That right there has taught me about teamwork as much as anything else my dad has said or done.

Once my dad and I were sitting together listening to a speaker address a large group. I was a little shocked when the speaker began giving basically one of my dad's talks. Without crediting Dad at all, the speaker used his outline, examples, quotes, scriptures, and even some of his jokes. I said, "Dad, aren't you going to go up and talk to him?" Dad just said, "We're all on the same team. We're all working toward the same goal."

I think of Joseph of old who was sold into Egypt. At a young age he had some prophetic dreams in which his family reverenced him. The scripture states that when Joseph told his family of the dreams, "His father rebuked him . . . and his brethren envied him" (Genesis 37:10–11). They, of all people, should have been the first to recognize that the Lord often speaks to his servants through dreams. Not only had Jacob been guided in dreams of his own, but their grandfathers had also been guided and promised blessings in dreams (see Genesis 26:24; 31:10, 24). Even though they and their families had been personally blessed in the fulfillment of dreams, they still chose to become angry with Joseph and envy him rather than include him on their team.

KEYS FOR ACTION

What Can We Do FOR Young People?

We can create environments in which young people need to work in teams. It can be as simple as having a group develop a skit or a cheer at a youth conference or as detailed as planning and carrying out a service project for the community. Anything that requires cooperation provides a great opportunity to teach teamwork.

However, the greatest lessons often happen on our way to the youth conference and service project, as we take time to get to know the young people who are involved. Make an effort to know names. God knows us individually by our names. When Heavenly Father appeared to Joseph Smith, he did not call, "Hey, you," or, "Aren't you one of the Smith boys?" He called him "Joseph."

We wish there were a secret memory trick or association game that worked every time to help us remember someone's name, but we have not found one. All we try to do is focus on the person and consciously make an effort. Then we repeat the name several times and whenever we get close enough to talk, we use the name again. When we see the person only once a week at church meetings, we write the name down inside a calendar or on a bookmark in our scriptures and that helps out. Helping a young person learn to remember a name and be able to call a person by it is something that will serve a young person well on a mission.

What Can We Do WITH Young People?

When dealing with people, the rule is to seek for similarities and learn from differences. If we think we have absolutely nothing in common with someone, we just need to look a little deeper. Once upon a time, that girl who acts so grown up and on top of things now was playing with Barbies. Once upon a time, that guy who seems so athletic and popular was playing with Teenage Mutant Ninja Turtles. When we start feeling out of place or intimidated, we can imagine the people who make us feel that way serving school lunch in elementary school. We can picture them with nets over their hair and big plastic aprons covering their clothes, the same as we once wore. Seeking similarities helps us to realize that at our cores we have a lot in common.

Along with finding similarities, we can learn from differences. When our family lived in New Zealand, visitors from the U.S. would say, "They drive on the wrong side of the road." We would laugh and respond, "They drive on the left side, but who says that is the wrong side?" In Latin America visitors would see two women walking hand in hand or arm in arm or greeting each other with a kiss on the cheek and say, "That's weird." We would laugh and reply, "It's not weird. It's just not what you are used to."

What Can Young People Do BY THEMSELVES?

One of the easiest ways to begin reaching out to others is to express thanks. Doctrine and Covenants 98:1 says, "In everything give thanks." When was the last time we thanked a leader? When was the last time we wrote a letter to a teacher who touched our hearts or a friend who was there at a turning point? It is easy to see the problems in our wards and feel frustrated because of members who are inactive or causing problems, but what about the faithful? Are we thanking them for not causing problems? When was the last time we thanked the deacon who passed us the sacrament? When was the last time we slipped a thank-you note in our fast-offering envelope for the clerk or member of the bishopric to find?

One missionary wrote to me: "One of the main things I have learned on my mission is that you can't do it alone. We have to acknowledge our dependence on God and Christ and we have to also learn to depend on each other and work together." Another success-ful elder was always expressing thanks to others. He would write little notes and tell people he appreciated them. He brightened many a day because he would "cease not to give thanks" (Ephesians 1:16). He fre-quently brightened my day and lifted my spirits by expressing his gratitude to me.

President Spencer W. Kimball was diligent about expressing appreciation. One man who worked in the Church welfare depart-ment counted up the thank-you notes he had received from the prophet through the years and they totaled twenty-nine! President Kimball routinely thanked associates, children, airport personnel, reporters, nurses, doctors—everyone. Once ten police officers surrounded a waiting car he was to enter, creating a human shield to protect him. President Kimball was told to get in the car quickly, but he wouldn't until he had thanked each of the officers personally for his help.[25]

Part Four:
ATTRIBUTES

▲ ▲ ▲

"Just as vital as what you do . . . is who you are. The restored
gospel enables you to become like Heavenly Father and
Jesus Christ. The Savior has shown the way."

Preach My Gospel, *115*

7

▲ ▲ ▲

BENEATH THE TIE

At the cultural event held before the rededication of the Santiago Temple, thousands gathered in a soccer stadium to hear the words of the prophet and see the young people perform. No one anticipated that the missionaries would also participate, but as the choir sang "Called to Serve," rows and rows of missionaries flooded out of one of the portals and marched across the field. Hundreds of missionaries wearing their white shirts and ties, blouses and skirts, and name tags were holding Chilean flags and waving to the crowd. Members and nonmembers alike were overcome by the sight, and many shed tears as they cheered for the elders, sisters, and couples who filled the field.

One member said, "Lots of sports and music stars have been met with cheers in that stadium, but nothing like what greeted the missionaries. They are the real heroes. It was a very emotional moment. It was like seeing angels."

All of us have had similar feelings of pride as we have watched missionaries in an airport or riding bikes down the street. They look clean-cut and wholesome. They stand out in refreshing contrast to those around them in the world.

Still, while missionaries can *look* good, it is more important that they *be* good. The Savior cursed the fig tree that looked good but didn't bear fruit (see Matthew 21:19). He condemned whited sepulchres, "which indeed appear beautiful outward, but are within full of dead men's bones, and of all uncleanness" (Matthew 23:27). When Jesus appeared to Joseph Smith, the Savior declared there were many "that draw near to me with their lips, but their hearts are far from me" (Joseph Smith—History 1:19). Missionaries need to be concerned about having neatly groomed hair, clean shoes, and conservative ties. But what really counts is what's beneath the tie.

One missionary explained: "I can't put on an act. I can't give the right answer and portray the right image when it's not real. I can't fake it. I have to be sincere." We have a new appreciation for the word *sincere* after learning Spanish. In Spanish *sin* means without and *cera* means wax. Long ago, when artisans would make items out of marble, if the marble had a flaw the seller would simply build it up or cover the imperfection with wax. This way the buyer would never know there was a problem until he would get it home, and the hot sun would melt the wax and expose the marble for what it was. So people started to ask, "Is this made *sin cera?*" Is this made without wax? They didn't want to buy something that looked wonderful but wouldn't hold up in the heat of the sun.

As we determine to live lives that are "without wax," we can reflect on our own personal worthiness having to do with living the Word of Wisdom, paying tithing, and observing the Sabbath day. Still, it is the breaking of the law of chastity that keeps more young people from their missions than anything else.

Too many young people discover too late that if you give Satan an inch, he'll take a mile. We have never heard anyone express regret for keeping the law of chastity—ever. On the other hand, we have heard many, many tearful expressions of remorse by those involved with fornication and adultery, including homosexual behavior, prostitution, and abuse and molestation of children. Such sins are extremely serious, but most people don't start there. They end up there because they have not made a consistent enough effort to control unworthy thoughts, discuss sexual topics with respect, avoid pornography and masturbation, and repent when they have slipped up.

CONTROLLING UNWORTHY THOUGHTS

President Ezra Taft Benson taught, "Our accountability begins with how we handle the evil thought immediately after it is presented."[26] That's comforting to know since in this wicked, telestial world, unbidden thoughts and ideas seem to demand room in our heads even when we have placed a "No Vacancy" sign in clear view. We don't seek them, invite them, or want them, but they still come. It's not our fault when a thought enters our heads. We just have to get rid of it before it takes up residence in our hearts.

The Savior warned, "Whosoever looketh on a woman to lust after her hath committed adultery with her already in his heart" (Matthew 5:28). And in the Old Testament we read, "As [a man] thinketh in his heart, so is he" (Proverbs 23:7).

Truman G. Madsen has suggested, "Reread the oft-quoted passages about the thoughts. You will note that it is not the occurrence of ideas in the head but their lodgment in the heart that degrades. . . . The issue is not so much what thoughts occur in our minds, but how we nurture them in our desires."[27]

Jesus gave the best advice of all when it comes to controlling our thoughts. He said, "If thy right hand offend thee, cut it off" (Matthew 5:30). *Offend* means to cause us to stumble. Christ was saying that if anything is causing us to stumble, we should get rid of it. That can include girlfriends or boyfriends who have a negative influence on us, as well as inappropriate activities, environments, and entertainment. Remember the people of Anti-Nephi-Lehi? They didn't just put away the weapons of war that had caused them to stumble. They *buried* them (see Alma 25:14).

When unworthy thoughts still appear, we cast them out by

replacing them with worthy ones. In Doctrine and Covenants 121:45 we read: "Let virtue garnish thy thoughts unceasingly; then shall thy confidence wax strong." Virtue is goodness. It is not enough to just try to empty our minds of evil or "dirty" thoughts. It is a matter of filling them with goodness, light, perspective, and purpose. With such things in mind, no wonder we can feel confident. If we are digging a hole in the backyard and we don't want the dirt to just get washed back in during the next rainstorm, we had better put something else in place of the dirt. In a similar way, we must replace inappropriate thoughts with virtuous thoughts.

Controlling our thoughts is easier to do when we keep ourselves physically active. Grandma Wilcox used to teach second grade, and she would always have the kids clap their hands or snap their fingers or move their bodies as she reviewed what they were learning. "If I engaged their bodies," she would say, "I focused their minds." We may not be second graders, but the principle still applies. We need to use that connection to our advantage. A wandering mind is rarely found in a moving body.

Dreams are perhaps one of the most misunderstood realms of thought. Now and then, most of us feel a little shocked by what we dream. It's okay to simply let it go, move on, and start the day in peace. Dreams are as uncontrollable as the constriction of our pupils when someone shines a bright light in our eyes. We cannot consciously will our pupils not to constrict. In the same way, we can't control our dreams and thus will not be held accountable for them.

When I served as mission president, missionaries would sometimes come to me quite concerned about nocturnal emissions. I would assure them that such dreams are normal and nothing to be ashamed of in any way. The elders felt bad because their dreams were graphic. I explained that they had to be in order to elicit a physical response from a sleeping body, similar to what we experience when we dream we are falling and we jerk and suddenly wake. Dreams are not brought on by unworthy thoughts or actions during the day. They are the body's natural way of providing a release when it is needed. I counseled the concerned elders that rather than feeling guilty they should instead thank Heavenly Father that their bodies were functioning normally.

When considering unworthy thoughts, keep a healthy perspective. Remember, many of the thoughts referred to as "bad" will someday, in the right place, at the right time, with the right person, be very good. Passions are not meant to be eliminated from our lives forever. They are simply meant to be bridled (see Alma 38:12). Appetites are not to be removed, but to be regulated. Desires are not to be ruled out, but to be ruled over. Thoughts are not to be conquered, but to be controlled.

DISCUSSING SEXUAL TOPICS WITH RESPECT

Russell's mission president taught his missionaries that human sexuality is a sacred thing and that any discussion of it is to be reverently approached. Just as we can't imagine the young men who prepare and dispose of the sacred emblems of the sacrament throwing the leftover bread at each other or stomping it into the dirt outside, we should also cringe at any irreverent or coarse references to the sacred powers of procreation God has granted us.

A temple sealing is also a sacred covenant and—though few think of it like this—sexual relations between a husband and wife are a symbol of that covenant. Joking about or making light of sex is as inappropriate and offensive as it would be to splash around in a baptismal font.

The topic of sex seems to come up everywhere in today's world, and young people naturally have a lot of questions. To ask our youth not to think about it or discuss it might be a little unrealistic. However, we do not hesitate in the least to ask that it be discussed appropriately and respectfully. We don't have to lower our language, humor, or actions to the gutter or locker-room level when talking about a sacred symbol of the covenant of marriage.

AVOIDING PORNOGRAPHY

Despite all the warnings from our prophet and leaders, some try to justify their interest in pornography. They may say, "It's just an art form." Wrong. Art in all of its forms can be sensuous (appealing to our senses) without being sensual (sexually stimulating and erotic).

Others rationalize, "It's just sex education." No way. In fact, it is sex mis-education because it is completely void of the commitment and emotional closeness that must accompany the physical act if there is to be any long-term satisfaction. Pornography teaches nothing about the responsibilities that accompany sex within a healthy marriage. Learning sex from pornography is like taking driver's education from a deaf and blind instructor. Not only would you have to question the accuracy of the information you would be getting, but letting such a teacher drive you around would be as dangerous as it would be stupid.

Still others claim, "I can view porn if I want. It's my life." Wrong again! Consider current family relationships and/or future marriage. Many people are affected by our choices. Pornography is not intimacy, but the illusion of intimacy. It is not love, but lust. It is not building, but destroying. Pornography is not real, but counterfeit. Those who choose to involve themselves in such a negative and selfish cycle affect all who love them and who are loved by them.

One elder had spent three years before his mission in the military. In that environment, he had been exposed to everything imaginable, but he stayed clean and strong. He said he knew guys who would spend their entire paychecks on pornography. How sad is that? He said that even good, Christian young men tried to justify their involvement with pornography by saying, "I'm just shopping around. Aren't you going to look around and then test-drive a car before you buy it?" Their reasoning shows how pornography had warped their thinking. Since when is a woman a car? Since when is a daughter of God nothing more than an object to be used, test-driven, and then purchased or cast aside?

Once a habit is established, change is possible. However, no one can do it alone. Viewing pornography is often done in private so addicts wrongfully believe they can break the habit in private. They can no sooner get out of quicksand on their own than break a pornography habit without help. The more they try, the deeper they sink. The only hope when stuck in quicksand is to reach out your arms and legs as far as they will go. This reaching out enables the victim to float until help arrives. The same is true for those sinking in the quicksand of pornography. They must reach out for help from their bishops, trusted friends and family members, and professionals. There are many steps that need to be taken in the long process of recovery, but the first and most important step is to reach out.

AVOIDING MASTURBATION

The world sees no harm in the practice of masturbation. It says it is a natural sexual outlet and a normal part of growing up. The truth is that for young men, nocturnal emissions provide the natural release for the body when such a release is necessary. That happens without stimulation. Many claim masturbation is okay because there are no physical consequences, but they are overlooking its serious emotional and spiritual consequences.

The practice can affect our ability to feel the Spirit and can lower self-esteem. It can cause feelings of depression and despair and lead to other problems including dishonesty and pulling away from others. The world would say that such feelings are a result of the guilt we feel because of an unreasonable standard imposed by the Church. They ignore the fact that guilt naturally accompanies bad choices whether or not the Church is involved. Everyone has the

Light of Christ, a conscience, and when we go against that light we experience guilt. The fact that the Church teaches that masturbation is wrong doesn't make it wrong. It is wrong because it is a selfish act that goes against the light. Even those who grow up without Church teachings still experience guilty feelings.

President Spencer W. Kimball affirmed that "God himself implanted the physical magnetism between the sexes for two reasons: for the propagation of the human race, and for the expression of that kind of love between man and wife that makes for true oneness."[28] Masturbation fills neither purpose. It does not allow for procreation, and the only love involved is strictly self-love. That kind of selfishness can have devastating effects in all aspects of our lives, but especially in marriage.

An upset man once said to me, "Bishops have no right to ask young people about something so private and personal. What does some old guy care if a kid is masturbating?"

What he didn't realize is that when such selfishness is allowed to go unchecked, it does not prepare a person for the realities of marriage, where one must be ready to give as well as take. A leader who is willing to ask about such a personal thing is showing that he truly cares about that young person's future. Young people who achieve self-mastery are better prepared to enter into a strong and satisfying marriage. Faithfulness within marriage deepens trust and engenders confidence. In such an environment love will bloom and the expression of love will bring a deep sexual satisfaction available only to those willing to pay the price.

I told the agitated man, "Consider the fact that one in every two marriages in the United States ends in divorce, yet in the Church it is much lower than that and among those who marry in the temple it is lower still. There may be lots of reasons, but perhaps one of them is that 'some old guy' cares enough about a kid's future happiness that he is willing to teach him self-control."

Controlling ourselves is like putting money in the bank. Those who never discipline themselves to make a deposit will never be able to make a withdrawal. Those who learn self-mastery early will always see positive returns on their investment.

For a young man who is struggling to overcome this habit, the key is to keep trying. It probably took a long time for him to fall into his current pattern, and breaking it will also take time. To promise to "never do it again" may be premature considering how long it has been a part of his life and how fast his body is producing to keep up with the demand. "Never again" may be the ultimate goal, but there are many smaller and more realistic goals that must be met first. A better promise to start with is that it is not going to happen without his talking to his bishop about it.

In *Preach My Gospel* we read, "Ideally, repenting of a specific sin should be necessary only once. However, if the sin is repeated, repentance is available as a means of healing. Repentance may involve an emotional and physical process. People must stop ongoing, ingrained ways of inappropriate acting. Undesirable actions must be replaced with healthy and appropriate behaviors. Thus, both repentance and recovery may take time."[29] No wonder President Boyd K. Packer referred to sincere repentance as "a pattern in our lives."[30]

Many who have been successful in breaking a masturbation habit started by separating masturbation from the viewing of pornography. Masturbating without viewing is a big step in the right direction. This has been followed by setting goals that allowed their bodies to slow down. Reaching a series of small, short-term goals has provided a feeling of success that built confidence and reinforced the belief that they could ultimately win. Many young men who have succeeded in overcoming this habit set goals in conjunction with their priesthood leader and reported back on their successes and failures. When nocturnal emissions began to happen, it was a good signal that the end was in sight because their bodies were slowing down and taking care of themselves. At that point their personal battle became a little easier. For these young men, change was not necessarily a quick process, but it was ultimately successful.

Some young women struggle in similar ways, but usually it is because there are emotional needs that are not being met as well as physical needs. Setting goals can also be appropriate and helpful for them.

For girls or boys, the bishop can be a valuable member of their support system. However, he is much more than that. He is the one authorized to receive their confession and can receive revelation in their behalf. He can give them priesthood blessings and inspired counsel. He can help them formulate a positive plan of action and use priesthood keys to assist them in their quest to resist temptation, repent, draw closer to the Savior, and claim the wonderful blessings of Jesus Christ's atonement. They will be amazed at the changes they can make when they stop relying on willpower alone and start relying on God's power.

REPENTANCE

Those who commit sexual sins feel terrible and sometimes begin to assume that there is no hope or reason to keep trying. The embarrassment, remorse, and guilt seem overwhelming. In an effort to rid himself of the guilt, the transgressor may look for an escape. Some try to hide their sin and pretend it didn't happen, or they try to rationalize that it wasn't that bad because "everyone does it." When that doesn't work, they sometimes try to blame others, laugh it off, or get angry. In extreme cases they try to convince themselves that God doesn't exist and that the standard for purity is arbitrary or simply man-made. Somehow they think that will eliminate the need to change. That kind of rationalization never works—at least not in the long run.

Caught in this dilemma, one elder said to me, "I don't believe there can be only one true church any more."

I told him, "That sounds like code for you've sinned and don't want to repent."

The young man was shocked and asked, "How can you say such a thing?" However, within a few weeks, the truth surfaced, and he approached me asking for help.

Guilt is to the spirit what pain is to the body. When we feel pain it is a clear signal to stop whatever we are doing that is hurting us physically. If we touch a hot stove, the pain makes us pull away. The ability to experience pain is a blessing because it keeps us from making things worse. No one in his right mind would say, "Even though this hurts, I am going to leave my hand on the stove and pretend it doesn't." Just like pain, guilt sends a strong signal to stop whatever we are doing that is hurting us spiritually.

President Boyd K. Packer writes:

> You may tell yourself that your transgressions are not spiritually illegal. That will not work; neither will rebellion, nor anger, nor joking about them. You cannot do that. And you don't have to do it. There is a way back. . . . Save for the exception of the very few who defect to perdition, there is no habit, no addiction, no rebellion, no transgression, no apostasy, no crime exempted from the promise of complete forgiveness. That is the promise of the Atonement of Christ.[31]

WHAT I TRIED

As much as we would like to keep our children sheltered from all temptations and worldly influences, it's impossible. We can't keep them in a box and feed them through a little hole in the top (although some parents have found that tempting). We must deal with children the way God deals with us. He loves us, prepares us, teaches us, and lets us decide what we will do and then face the natural consequences. Heavenly Father doesn't stop the storms from coming. He simply offers us a refuge from the storm. We can't shelter our children completely, but we can offer a support system—an umbrella against the rain. My wife and I try to do this by being informed and interested.

Debi and I have attempted to become knowledgeable about drinking, drugs, gambling, and gangs. We have read about Internet dangers, pornography, and sexual abuse. If issues are raised in general conference or in the *For the Strength of Youth* pamphlet that we don't know much about, we seek additional information. We are far from being experts, but we know enough to watch for signs of early involvement.

Debi and I visit our children's schools. When the kids were younger we volunteered to help in their classrooms. Now that they are older, we stay involved by helping with activities or attending events. We know our way around the buildings. The principals and faculty members know us. We see what the students are wearing (or not wearing, as the case may be), what the tone is in the hallways, and what the language is like. We have felt it important to know what our children are facing every day.

Along with being informed, we must show interest. When I began my service as mission president, some missionaries were not in the habit of writing their regular weekly letters to the president. Reminders of the requirement did little to motivate a change. However, when the missionaries realized that not only was I reading the letters but I was highlighting parts and bringing them to interviews to discuss with them, the number of letters increased dramatically. Soon everyone was sending weekly letters. As they gained confidence that the letters were confidential, the number of details they shared also increased. When the missionaries discovered I was interested, the communication soared.

The same thing can happen with our children. Obviously they

don't write a weekly letter to us, but the quantity and quality of their communications will improve when they know they can talk to us and we are going to listen and not get upset. One young man said to me, "I would like to talk with my dad about girls and stuff because he is a guy, and I think he would understand, but I don't ever feel like he has time for me. When I say, 'Dad, can we talk?' he just rolls his eyes, looks at his watch, and says, 'Well, okay. So what's so important that we have to talk about it right now?' It totally kills my enthusiasm."

In our home, my wife and I ask what is going on and don't settle for the typical response of "Nothing!" We've tried to keep doors of communication open at mealtimes and other group settings, but also in private. I've always heard of fathers who do personal priesthood interviews with their children. I admire that, but such formality is not my style. I just talk to them when we are alone in the car together or have a special date. Debi finds the best times to speak to them are when they get home from school and when they are getting settled in for sleep.

If we want our children to be able to talk to us about big things—doubts, fears, and temptations—we have to be willing to listen to the small things—stress at school, why the team lost the game, friends who hurt their feelings, and so forth. Still, if the bigger issues are not coming up naturally, I bring them up myself. My children have had to get used to some pretty direct questions. I don't interrogate my kids, and I certainly don't ask more than one or two questions at a time, but I do regularly look for private moments when I can ask: Has anyone offered you drugs? Have you ever tasted alcohol? Has anyone ever touched you in private places? When was the last time you saw pornography? How are you doing on controlling your thoughts? What do you do when you hear a dirty joke? Are you involved with masturbation? What is your biggest struggle or temptation? How are your prayers? How strong is your testimony?

If problems surface, we can talk about them. If no problems

come up, I can compliment them and express my gratitude and pride. Most of all, I hope that by my asking specific questions, they know that I am informed and interested. I want them to know that I am part of that umbrella and not the storm.

RUSSELL'S RESPONSE

Dad and his questions—I have to laugh. There we would be, working in the yard or washing dishes, and all of a sudden he would whip out, "So, when was the last time you saw pornography?" I would always say, "Dad, you have been a bishop for too long! You really need a different calling!" Still, I have to admit that his questions served his purpose. I did know my parents knew about the issues facing youth. I also knew that Dad would be asking me about these issues, and that kept me on my toes.

I just never know what is going to come out of my dad's mouth. He is pretty blunt and straightforward about sexual things. Don't get me wrong. He is not crude. He just calls a spade a spade. I have learned to appreciate that because discussing sex and getting my questions answered took away the curiosity and mystery so I wasn't as tempted to experiment.

In Alma 12:32 we read, "Therefore God gave unto them commandments, after having made known unto them the plan of redemption." A lot of parents give rules, but I liked how my parents would explain why. For example, my parents didn't just tell me that pornography was evil or dirty and stop there. They also told me how pornography could mess up my life and ruin my future marriage. They said pornography weakens the trust, love, and commitment that are essential for a healthy sexual relationship in marriage. I decided that when I got married I wanted my wife to be able to trust me. I wanted to enjoy a positive sexual relationship with her and have a healthy and happy marriage. That gave me a good reason to make the choice to avoid pornography.

When I was younger I loved reading about the time when Nephi burst the bonds with which his brothers bound him. With strength and faith he was made free (see 1 Nephi 7:15–17). For those who struggle with bad habits, Nephi's story can have additional meaning. Satan is our brother and, like Laman and Lemuel, he seeks to bind us with chains of sin, doubt, selfishness, and pride. Some pray that temptations will be taken away. God could break the chains, but that would rob us of the opportunity to build strength for the future. Perhaps this is why Peter teaches, "The trial of your faith [is] much more precious than of gold" (1 Peter 1:7).

Dad talks about providing an umbrella for the storm. The best umbrella is ultimately Jesus. He is our safe shelter. In Psalms there is a beautiful scripture about Jesus: "The Lord is my rock, and my fortress, and my deliverer; my God, my strength, in whom I will trust; my buckler, and the horn of my salvation, and my high tower" (Psalm 18:2). When I first read that passage I was impressed by how many powerful lessons were taught about the Savior in one short verse, but there was one I didn't understand. *What is a buckler?* I thought. My grandma would be proud that I actually used the dictionary she had given me. As I flipped the pages to *buckler* I found that it is, "a shield used for parrying." That naturally led me forward a few pages in the dictionary to find out that *parrying* means to divert a blow of any type. Jesus is our buckler, our shield that diverts all the blows of life, be they insults, arguments, fights, or temptations.

KEYS TO ACTION

What Can We Do FOR Young People?

When I was a bishop in a student ward, I began to notice an interesting pattern as young people would come to me to discuss problems. It seemed that many problems started at sleepovers when the participants were younger. That's where these young people were being introduced to pornography, drinking, vandalism, sexual experimentation, masturbation, and even homosexual behaviors. Several young women spoke of sexual molestation and abuse that haunted them for years that had occurred at the hands of an older male when they were at a sleepover at a girlfriend's home. One wise young man explained, "Nothing very good ever happens at sleepovers, even if you are with other LDS kids."

We realize the experience of these young people cannot be generalized to everyone. Still, it seemed more than a coincidence that so many had sexual experiences at sleepovers. It was enough of an eye-opener for me that I told my own children their sleepover days were over. The children still liked to play late with neighborhood and ward friends, but they came home to sleep. We have attended family reunions where kids have slept with cousins, but in large groups and under adult supervision similar to a well-planned Scout camp or youth conference. In this way we have tried to avoid problems.

What Can We Do WITH Young People?

The Internet is useful in many positive ways. Staying in touch with family and friends by e-mail and having easy access to material related to the Church can strengthen us in our resolve to live our standards. It can also be a big help in school. But everyone knows there are also Internet drawbacks and dangers: pornography, chat rooms, anti-Mormon sites, gambling, and on-line games not only can waste time and money, but they can also affect lives in ways that are devastating.

Parents can install protection programs and passwords, but these are not an iron-clad guarantee. One young man said, "If parents think their children are safe just because they bought some program, they'd better think again. There are lots of ways around the programs, and you can always find a computer someplace that doesn't have any safeguards." We have to focus on other ways to protect ourselves.

Here are some of the things Debi and I have done in an effort to keep our children safe: Keep computers in high-traffic areas and post pictures of Christ and temples by the computer. Limit time spent on the computer. There are other interests and activities that can be equally productive and entertaining. Check computer records. One girl said, "Some people call it snooping, but my mom just calls it 'good, old-fashioned parenting.'" Supervise any off-line meetings with strangers. Before such meetings take place, there are almost always phone calls involved. Check bills for unfamiliar numbers. If young people really want to meet someone off-line for any reason, be sure to accompany them and meet at a public place, never at home.

Nothing is going to be more helpful for young people than for parents to ask questions and speak openly about Internet dangers. Most teenagers appreciate it when parents approach them in private and ask point-blank questions about Internet use. It helps them when parents ask for promises about what will or will not be done on the Internet. One young man explained, "My parents used to have a screening system, but it was really messing things up because it would block sites that shouldn't have been blocked. It wouldn't even let us look up DeseretBook.com, so we finally removed it. That's when my parents told me that the best filter is the Holy Ghost. They put the responsibility on me and asked me to commit to staying clear of the bad stuff. That helped me a lot." A young woman related, "My parents asked me to promise them I wouldn't go into chat rooms. They trust me, and I don't want to lose that trust." Another young man recounted, "When I left for college this past year, my parents asked me to promise them I would make smart decisions when I got to the dorms and had access to computers without safety programs. That promise has been the best safety program ever."

What Can Young People Do BY THEMSELVES?

One elder wrote to me, "Dear President, You have no idea how much I would have liked to never tell another soul the things I told you. I have kept them hidden and covered for so long, and I tried to convince myself that it was just between God and me, but I knew I had to share them with you. I felt a heavy burden all week before I talked with you. Then the miracle occurred. I've learned about the Atonement all my life, but now I felt it change my life. I was giving my burden to the Lord, and I felt an intense peace take the place of my pain. I had read in Job about how our sins could go away like water in a river, and I longed for that. Now I feel it has happened. President, I feel free and, oh, how great it is to feel free from these sins of the past that have tormented me for years."

In the Old Testament we read, "He that covereth his sins shall not prosper: but whoso confesseth and forsaketh them shall have mercy" (Proverbs 28:13). In the Doctrine and Covenants the Lord says, "I . . . forgive sins unto those who confess their sins" (64:7). Confession is only part of the repentance process, but it is an important part that must not be overlooked. The only sins the Atonement can't cover are those we choose to keep hidden.

Does God need us to outline each detail of our sins because he was taking a little nap during the last party we attended? No. After Adam and Eve partook of the forbidden fruit, God asked them questions: "Where goest thou?" "Who told thee thou wast naked?" "What is this thing which thou hast done?" (Moses 4:15–19). Did God really need answers to such questions? Did he want responses for his sake or, as a wise and masterful teacher, did he want the question answered for the sake of Adam and of Eve? Heavenly Father does not need knowledge or enlightenment. His children do. God does not need our confession as much as we need to confess.

"But it's scary," young people say again and again. It *can* be a little frightening when we finally face our deepest weaknesses and most debased actions. After their transgression, even the noble Adam and Eve were afraid—they "went to hide themselves from the presence of the Lord God amongst the trees of the garden" (Moses 4:14). But could the trees hide them? Could their fig-leaf aprons? (see Moses

4:13). No more than our silence, avoidance, and procrastination can conceal our deeds and thoughts from God's all-seeing eyes.

However frightening confession may be, it is done for the sake of the transgressor, and it gives him or her the chance to receive forgiveness from the Church, covenant to change, and receive help, counsel, and guidance in making the change.

One of the saddest interviews I conducted as a mission president was a final interview with an elder who, instead of talking about goals for the future, finally gave a full confession of some things that had occurred before his mission. He had not dared bring these things up before for fear of not being allowed to serve or of being sent home. The truth is that nothing he said was of such a serious nature that either option would have been the case. I was sad that this missionary had carried these preoccupations so needlessly through his entire mission. I was sad that the boy didn't have more spiritual maturity and godly sorrow earlier. Most of all, I felt bad that this young man who had been teaching about Christ his entire mission had failed to understand that the blessings he promised others were also there for him.

The Hebrew translation of the word *atonement* is *Kaphar,* which means "to cover." In the Garden of Eden, after Adam and Eve confessed and made promises to change, "The Lord God, [did] make coats of skins, and clothed them" (Moses 4:27). As we confess—exposing our honest actions and innermost selves—and make positive changes, the Lord will do for us what he did for Adam and Eve. In confession we bare our souls, uncover our past, and demonstrate our humility. In that moment when feelings of imperfection, inadequacy, shame, and embarrassment are most intense—when we have, as it were, a "perfect knowledge of all our guilt, and our uncleanness, and our nakedness"—the Lord will clothe us. He will attire us in peace, joy, and forgiveness, just as he will ultimately array us in "robe[s] of righteousness" (2 Nephi 9:14) and "garments of salvation" (Isaiah 61:10). He will re-dress us with his Spirit. In Christ's atonement we are, most literally, covered.

The coats of skins—the only thing Adam and Eve were able to take with them from the Garden of Eden—covered them physically. However, they also became tangible and powerful reminders of the Atonement. They were made of the skins of animals that were sacrificed just as the Savior would one day be sacrificed that we might all be covered spiritually. We, like Adam and Eve, will be able to face our Father clothed and unashamed because Jesus has us covered.

8

▲ ▲ ▲

LISTENING WITH LOVE

What's wrong with this picture? Two missionaries show up at a door. The woman who answers their knock recognizes them as being religious. She tells them about how she once prayed to be made well and how God healed her. One of the elders responds, "We have a message to share with you about eternal families."

Another woman has received several lessons but feels nervous when the missionaries speak about baptism. Although her father has passed away, she still feels like she would be insulting his memory by joining a different church. After explaining her feelings, a missionary says, "But I know that Joseph Smith was the prophet of the Restoration."

A couple has lived together for many years without being married. The sister missionaries have just taught them the law of chastity. The man says, "We are a lot happier together than many married couples I know." One of the sisters responds, "That's impossible because wickedness never was happiness."

All of these examples have one thing in common: the missionaries weren't listening—not really. They were so focused on what they had to say that they didn't hear what was being said, and they certainly didn't respond appropriately or with sensitivity. They wanted to talk so people would listen rather than listen so people would talk.

They wanted to be understood without being willing to be understanding.

One elder who served in Chile was asked what he had learned on his mission. He said, "You don't always have to be talking. You can listen. That's usually when you feel inspiration come. I thought I came on my mission to speak, teach, and preach, but now that my mission is drawing to a close I realize I did my best work by listening."

Listening is one of the most powerful elements in building and maintaining relationships. We must hear the words, hear between the words, and hear beyond the words.

THE WORDS

We are all familiar with the world-changing scripture found in James 1:5: "If any of you lack wisdom, let him ask of God." Sometimes we forget there is more that follows. In that same chapter we read some additional counsel that, if heeded, could also change the world: "Wherefore, my beloved brethren, let every man be swift to hear, slow to speak, slow to wrath" (James 1:19).

It is far too easy to rush in and try to solve the problem, give the "correct answer," or fill the air with advice. Effective listening requires time, intent, and a temporary suspension of judgment. We don't need to interrupt or defend ourselves too soon. When feelings are running high, people need to be heard. We can nod, rephrase, or provide a soft "um-hum" to acknowledge that we have heard. We must turn off the TV, phone, and laptop. We need to close the catalog or newspaper and open our ears.

Does that mean we are simply supposed to sit there with our mouths shut? We might try it more often. It's surprising to see the quality and quantity of comments that can be drawn out of people by silence. Wise bishops know this. They don't simply ask, "How are you?" and settle for a quick, "Fine." They wait in silence to hear more, and they usually do.

When people are upset or discouraged, they don't need solutions and scripture references as much as they need sympathetic sounding boards. Usually being allowed to vent the feelings we are "not supposed to be feeling" is the first step toward moving beyond those negative emotions. As we develop listening skills, what we are really developing is patience, tolerance, and true acceptance of others. We are learning how to show our love. Heavenly Father shows his love by listening to our prayers. In fact, as we pray, he usually does quite a bit more listening than talking.

BETWEEN THE WORDS

Often, the most important part of communication is to hear what isn't being said. A UCLA study that resulted in what is known as Mehrabian's Rule points out that the average person hears only about seven percent of what is said with words. Another fifty-five percent of what is communicated comes from body language, and thirty-eight percent comes from the tone of voice. So along with listening with our ears, we must listen with our minds. True attitudes and feelings are usually expressed through gestures, posture, rate of speech, volume, and eye placement.

We have all seen a speaker who is shaking so uncomfortably at the pulpit that the microphone wobbles. Yet the first words out of his mouth are usually, "I'm so happy to be here today." It is pretty easy to see that he is communicating with more than his words. It is the same with the greeter in a wedding reception line who says, "So glad you came," all the while looking over our shoulders to the next people in line. Once a visitor came to our home, and when we thanked her for coming, she said, "There is no place I would rather be." Nice thought, but her constant checking of her watch and looking out the window communicated a different message.

When listening to someone, we need to notice the expression on his face, the look in his eyes, the way he holds his head. We can detect boredom, hostility, or fatigue simply by observing the fidgeting of people's legs and the movement of their hands. Watch carefully for nonverbal signals.

Listening is like caring for a crying baby. We don't always know why he is upset. We just know he is. We try changing him and still he cries. We try feeding him and that doesn't work. We try rocking him and nothing helps. We think, *Why aren't you older so you could just tell me what is wrong?*

Many teens, missionaries, and adults don't express their real needs and desires any better now than they did when they were babies. It is still up to us to hear them cry and try to identify and meet the need.

One young woman wrote, "I think there are things wrong with me. Deep inside there is someone crying for help, but I have built a wall and locked out everyone who tries to help. I don't cry any more—at least not on the outside."

Elder Marvin J. Ashton of the Quorum of the Twelve Apostles once said, "I hear . . . people crying to us when they don't even know they are crying."[32] LDS composer Kenneth Cope wrote a song in which he counsels, "Hear them cry the tears they hide. Love means time. Hear them cry."[33] As we develop the ability to hear between the words, what is really being demonstrated is social awareness, concern, tact, and generosity.

BEYOND THE WORDS

Along with listening with our ears and minds, we have to learn to listen with our hearts. It is easy to love the loveable. It is pleasant to love those who love us. However, Jesus said, "For if ye love them which love you, what reward have ye? do not even the publicans the same? And if ye salute your brethren only, what do ye more than others?" (Matthew 5:46–47).

But how do we love someone who has lied to us or failed to live up to the simplest of commitments? How do we love someone who has hurt us and bad-mouthed us to everyone? How do we love someone who has pulled away and will not even speak to us? How do we love a person who is covered with chains, tattoos, and weird symbols, or who is dressed all in black with a strange hairstyle?

There may not be a sure-fire answer to cover every unique situation, but it does help to hear the secret message. It is one thing to listen to the message (the words), another to hear the complete message (between the words), and still another to hear the secret message (beyond the words).

A guest speaker was once addressing a Relief Society conference to which the Young Women had also been invited. No sooner had the sister begun her talk than she noticed three young women talking quietly to one another. She felt resentful. She was used to receiving full attention when she spoke. She paused and waited until the offenders noticed. Then she smiled at them and continued. To her surprise, the girls kept whispering to one another. The speaker's resentment grew. She thought, *Why did they come if they don't want to hear what I have to say?* She stopped again and stared right at them and this time didn't smile. Surely they would understand her message. However, the minute she began speaking again, they also began. Their conversation was quieter, but not totally squelched. The speaker finally gave up trying to get their attention and simply finished her talk. Inside she felt frustrated and wished that whoever had made these girls come had just let them stay home.

After the talk, as all who attended were enjoying refreshments in the cultural hall, a woman approached the speaker and said, "I hope those girls didn't disturb you too much. . . . They've only been in the country a week. . . . They don't speak English very well. They were sitting there trying to help one another figure out what you were saying."

The speaker suddenly saw beyond perception and judgment into reality. She no longer wanted to take the girls and shake them by the shoulders. Instead, she wanted to take them in her arms and tell them how glad she was that they had come. Suddenly, she knew their secret, and it changed everything.[34]

When someone lies to us or lets us down, we can look for the secret. What has happened in his life to make him act this way? When someone gossips, look for the secret. What has made that person so insecure? What kind of pain has been dealt with to cause such low self-esteem? When someone has pulled away rejecting the very expressions of love that are so needed, look for the secret. What has made her feel so angry, alone, and devalued? When people offend with their extreme dress and behavior, look for the secret. Who has hurt them so deeply that they would build such a high wall to protect themselves?

In the hymn "Lord, I Would Follow Thee," Susan Evans McCloud writes, "In the quiet heart is hidden sorrow that the eye can't see."[35] Perhaps that sorrow can't be seen with our eyes, but it can be discovered with our ears, our minds, and our hearts. Even if we never know the secret (and often it is not even our place to know), the mere act of looking for it opens the door to understanding, and what we can understand, we can begin to love.

Sorrows, emotional pain, and life's unfairness don't excuse negative behavior—be it lying, backbiting, rudeness, inappropriate attention-getting, or gossiping. Still, though they don't excuse it, they do explain it. It is not required of any of us to love the sin, just the sinner. Knowing the secret softens us and helps us keep perspective so we can do just that.

As we develop the ability to hear beyond the words, we are actually developing empathy, long-suffering, and charity. These attributes give us hope in even the most desperate situations. That vision, plus lots of time and the power of the Savior's atonement, can not only help us recognize hidden sorrows but also help us see them healed.

WHAT I TRIED

Sometimes we listen for the purpose of enjoyment—such as listening to music. Sometimes we listen for information—such as during a news broadcast or in a class. Other times we must listen critically and discriminately in order to protect ourselves. But there are also times to listen empathetically and therapeutically. Perhaps the biggest challenge is knowing when a certain type of listening is required. For example, a teacher is going to expect more than the nodding of your head or an "um-hum" when she asks a direct question. If someone wants directions to a particular address, it would be inappropriate to respond by saying, "Let me see if I understand where you're coming from. I can tell it's important for you to know how to find this address." What if someone dials our phone number by accident? We don't need to respond in a rude or curt manner, but it is not a time for therapeutic listening. Similarly, if someone is trying to convince us to invest our life savings in a "sure thing" that "can't fail," it is no time for empathy.

Nevertheless, there are other times when people are seeking to share their feelings and asking for nothing except our time, sympathy, and interest. In such moments, they don't need a lecture. They just need a friend.

My wife, Debi, is good listener. I think she learned it from her mother, who is also a wonderful listener. I'm afraid I am still learning. It's pretty easy for me to rush in and try to solve the problem ("Tell him to knock it off") or fill the air with advice ("You shouldn't care what others think of you"). When my daughter says, "I'm so sick of school!" my immediate response is to remind her how blessed she is to have the opportunity to get a good education ("There are kids in Africa . . ."). When a family member is wallowing in self-pity I want to sing, "Count your blessings." It's my wonderful wife who reminds me to hold my tongue. Under the table she steps on my toe or pinches my leg as a reminder to just be quiet. The things I want to say may be helpful at another time and in another place, but not in the moment when someone has opened up and shared some honest, heart-felt experiences. Thank heaven for a wife who is teaching me to listen, by example—and also by pinching me under the table.

RUSSELL'S RESPONSE

I've always wondered why my father limps after every meal. Wow! Look at what I am learning!

Throughout this chapter, we have noted some of the attributes developed and demonstrated by good listening: patience, tolerance, acceptance, generosity, love, empathy, and charity. That is already quite a wonderful list, but I think there is another item: humility.

More than anything else, I believe listening takes and teaches humility. Once, my mom and dad really misjudged me. They made some generalizations without all the facts. It didn't happen often, but that time they came down on me unfairly. They were assuming something that wasn't true and expecting something I was unwilling to do. I got angry and left the house, slamming the door behind me. Even though it was late, I drove around for a long time. I felt misunderstood, angry, and frustrated. I love my parents, but that night I wanted to trade them in for an upgrade. In the morning I still felt mad. I didn't speak to them when I saw them. They were treating me like a little kid, and I felt I deserved better. I had been hurt and wanted to make them admit they were wrong. The tone in the house was far from what it should be.

As the day wore on, I realized that as wrong as I felt my parents had been, I was wrong, too. I wasn't being humble. I kept replaying their unfair words over and over in my mind without listening beyond them. As I tried to understand why they had said what they had, I could see why my mom and dad were concerned. I could see how they had previously been hurt by people who did similar things. They were assuming I would also hurt them. All night I had interpreted their involvement as meddling and controlling, but now I was also seeing it as evidence that they cared for and loved me. I went home with a different attitude, a less judgmental attitude.

I told my parents I was sorry. They apologized, too. It had been a long night and a hard day for all of us, but everything changed when I stopped worrying about which of us was right or wrong and just started being more humble.

Were my parents wrong? Yes and no. Was I wrong? Yes and no. Isn't that the way it always goes? The point is that pride blocked communication completely. Humility opened the door.

KEYS FOR ACTION

What Can We Do FOR Young People?

I Don't Have to Make Everything All Better. Not only is that the title of a wonderful book by our friends Gary and Joy Lundberg, but it is also a powerful reminder that our responsibilities have limits.[36] The Lundbergs teach that when someone expresses feelings or frustrations, we can validate the emotions by saying, "I understand that must be difficult" or "I can't imagine going through that." Then, instead of offering advice or a solution, we can simply ask, "What are you going to do about it?"

Sooner or later, people can usually figure out the next step to take without our spelling it out for them. When visiting with some who have allowed themselves to slip into inactivity in the Church, we have often found them anxious to talk about why. They vent about the injustices and unfairness they have suffered or how offended they have been.

Over and over, we have wanted to rush to the defense of priesthood leaders and the Church. Over and over, we have wanted to open the scriptures and read them the warnings. But we are usually most successful when we stifle those initial desires and simply ask, "What are you going to do about it?" and then offer the support, help, and encouragement they need to reach their goals.

What Can We Do WITH Young People?

In our conversations with young people, we are sometimes willing to listen, but no one is sharing any personal feelings. Let's face it—when you ask, "How's it going?" and someone says, "Great, just great," there is not much empathetic listening required. Now and then, we need to invite more by asking questions. Remember that conversations have to build to a point in which the following questions would be appropriate, but once we have established a good relationship and achieved a level of trust, we can ask such things as: What's most important to you? Do you ever feel like something is missing in your life? Have you ever wondered why God allows so much suffering? If you could ask God one question, what would it be? If you could have anything you want, what would you wish for?

When we wish to be empathetic and convey a spiritual message, it is sometimes effective to start by sharing something important to us and then following the statement with a question: To me the gospel of Jesus Christ brings joy. What brings you joy in your life? I find peace in worship. How do you and your family worship and find peace? Starting meaningful conversations in this way helps set a pattern young people can follow when they are missionaries.

What Can Young People Do BY THEMSELVES?

Remember that nobody is perfect. We appreciate the Japanese philosophy of imperfection: *wabi sabi* (wah'-bee sah'-bee), which implies that someone's intentions can be good even if the execution isn't. Next time someone preaches at us instead of really listening, we can take a deep breath and think to ourselves *wabi sabi*. See the person's efforts, however imperfect, as evidence that he or she cares. Next time a Church leader isn't especially sensitive or understanding, think *wabi sabi*. His intentions were honorable. As we cut others some slack, perhaps they will do the same for us. When we fail to listen as well as we should, perhaps others will be kind enough to walk away from us muttering *wabi sabi*.

Part Five:

SKILLS

▲ ▲ ▲

"Do all you can to leave your area stronger than you found it. . . . You will . . . be expected to devote all your time and attention to serving the Lord."

Preach My Gospel, *137*

"Be more bold in opening your mouth. . . . Seek to talk with everyone you meet. . . . Be warm, friendly, and cheerful."

Preach My Gospel, *156–57*

9

▲ ▲ ▲

"GET OUT THERE AND ASTONISH SOMEONE!"

Shortly before Elder Jeffrey R. Holland left Chile after directing the work there for two years, he arranged to speak to the missionaries. It was an unforgettable occasion for the elders and sisters present who got to meet Elder and Sister Holland and hear their messages. Sister Holland assured them they were not alone in the work and that they received much help from unseen sources. Elder Holland spoke about the Book of Mormon and the Atonement and ended his talk by saying, "This gospel is astonishing. Now get out there and astonish someone!"

Their words motivated and emboldened the missionaries who were anxious to apply the counsel. A few days later, one elder talked to a man on a bus and requested his address so they could share a message with his entire family. The man said he had enjoyed their visit but declined to give his address. The elder mustered all his courage and said, "Sir, you have no idea what you are missing. This message could change your family for generations to come." The man presented the elder with his address. The man had been astonished.

A sister missionary and her companion were teaching a young family. As they testified of dispensations, apostasy, and the Restoration, the man's head was swimming. When they introduced the Book of Mormon the man could no longer remain silent. He blurted out, "Do you realize what you are saying?"

The sisters said, "Yes!"

He said, "I mean you really have something here. This could revolutionize the world of religion completely. How come no one knows about this? You've gotta tell people!"

The sister missionary said, "That's what we are trying to do! That's why we are talking to you." The man had been astonished.

Another missionary was heading home with his companion and felt prompted to knock at a door. It was late in the evening, and the man who answered said he didn't have time for the Mormons. The elder offered to explain why people call us Mormons in less than two minutes. The man was curious, so the elder proceeded. When he finished the man said, "Jesus Christ in the Americas? Prophets in our day? Do you know what this means if it is true?"

The elder replied, "Oh, yeah!" The man, who originally didn't have time for the Mormons, set an appointment to have them return the following day. He had been astonished.

Another pair of elders was heading home at the end of a long day. Ahead they saw a man pushing his broken-down car. Neither missionary really wanted to help, but they knew they should and hurried to catch up. They pushed the car to a gas station, where the man thanked them and said, "I'm not a member of your church, but my wife and son are. In fact, my son who was steering the car as we pushed was just made a deacon. When the car stalled, I told him there was no way I could push it alone. He said, 'Don't worry, Dad. I prayed that Heavenly Father would send some elders to help. They should be along soon.'" The man definitely had been "astonished exceedingly" (Alma 20:26). So had the elders!

These missionaries and others took Elder Holland's challenge and witnessed the difference it made. They weren't moving mountains—as astonishing as that would be. But they were doing something much more important. They were moving people closer to God.[37]

What keeps us from doing the same? What keeps us from being bold and confident as we declare the truths of the gospel to the world? There may be many deterrents, but one is definitely fear.

A sister wrote, "I have lived with my fears for so long that they have built up and defined who I am. I don't know what I expected when I signed up to be a missionary. I think I figured that when I got set apart it would magically make me speak more and feel more comfortable with people. When that didn't happen I couldn't understand why. I had this image of the missionary I would be and when she didn't appear I got frustrated. Then, slowly, I began to see the big picture, and I realized there was something more I needed to do rather than wallow in my insecurities. I had a sector with lots of potential. In doing the work I'd been sent to do even though I was not perfect at it (or even very good at it), I began to find that other things didn't matter as much. The fears I had lived with for so long faded out of my life. I discovered who I am without the fears."

Like this sister, we all feel afraid at times. We wonder if we really have what it takes. We don't want to be rejected, teased, or embarrassed in front of other people. How did this sister overcome her fears? How can all of us face and conquer ours? Following are a few keys.

PURPOSE PROVIDES POWER

This sister called it seeing the big picture. She realized her purpose was more important than her fears. It's the same thing that a young mother realized when she was in a college class discussing fear. Upon admitting she was terrified of heights, the teacher asked, "So, would you ever venture out onto the ledge of a tall building?"

"Never."

The teacher asked, "What if your child were out there and you needed to save him?"

The mom immediately said, "If my child were in danger I would do anything." Everyone in the class was amazed at how quickly she could go from "never" to "anything." The difference came from seeing a bigger picture.

President Gordon B. Hinckley wrote, "Self discipline . . . virtue . . . obedience to commandments. . . . These may be difficult but they are possible under the motivation that comes of an understanding of truth."[38]

At Jesus' death his apostles were disoriented. After years of being sustained and uplifted by Christ's presence, they were on their own, confused and afraid. What changed these frightened apostles into confident, heroic leaders who changed the world? There is but one answer—the sure knowledge that Christ had risen from the grave. They knew that death—the universal enemy of mankind—had been defeated. That message was of greater importance than their fears. Their grasp of that larger picture changed them and us forever.

One of the elders who served with us in Chile said, "I've learned to overcome my fears, and the mission has been the perfect place to do it. The truth we teach has given me the power to stop hiding."

EXPECT THE BEST

We sometimes hesitate to initiate a conversation with strangers for fear of what others might think. But the truth is, others aren't usually paying that much attention. Most people are simply too worried about themselves to really spend much time analyzing or critiquing us. We worry about whether our hair is in place, our clothes are just right, and if our words are coming out as we planned. All the while those around us are usually so worried about themselves that they don't give us a second thought.

One missionary said, "In the mission I have found out I have a voice. I can bring things to the table that are unique and valuable. I stopped worrying about what others might say or think."

Another missionary said, "I used to think that 'they' wouldn't want to hear me or 'they' would make fun of my ideas. But 'they' isn't even a real person. Since realizing that, I'm not as quiet as I used to be. I can look people in the eyes and make friends."

SEE THROUGH PERSECUTION

One young woman said, "One of my friends watches me like a hawk—especially because I'm Mormon. She's always bugging me, cutting me low, or making some rude remark about my standards."

It is important to expect the best and realize that most people aren't going to tease, but there are always those few who enjoy being the exception to any rule. When those characters start to belittle, we need to see through their actions.

When people ridicule, bully, reject, or exclude, it is often because they don't feel good about themselves. Elder Vaughn J. Featherstone wrote, "The mature individual includes all, the insecure person excludes others as a way of building his or her own image. But everyone can see through it. It is fake and empty and unkind."[39]

One missionary wrote, "I have been spat on, yelled at, hosed down, and have even had people throw rocks at me. Not every day, but it has happened. When these things have occurred, I just always thought about how people persecuted the Savior, and I said inside my mind, 'Father, forgive them, for they know not what they do.'"

ACT WITH CONFIDENCE

Missionaries must act with confidence even when they don't feel confident. An elder from Argentina said, "I arrived in the mission afraid to talk to people. I really had to pray for courage. It literally hurt inside I felt so uncomfortable talking to strangers. My companions pushed me to do it, and each time I did I felt good after. I felt better about myself each time I stretched." By the end of his mission, not only had the elder overcome his own fear, but he was a trainer and leader in the mission helping others do the same.

President Gordon B. Hinckley wrote, "There is something about a mission that is different from all the other experiences of our lives. . . . You go out green as grass, and in about three months you mature in a miraculous and wonderful way. Your fears leave you. You're not afraid to go up and knock on a door. That is a terrible thing the first time you try it, but your fears leave you. You are able to stand in a street meeting . . . [and] there comes into your heart a new assurance and a new boldness to do that which you ought to do."[40]

REPLACE FEAR WITH FAITH

In the third verse of the hymn "Do What Is Right," we are encouraged to "be faithful and fearless."[41] Along with telling us what to do, perhaps this text is also reminding us how to do it, for we can indeed be more fearless as we are more faithful.

Another elder from Argentina and serving in Chile said, "I came to the mission very shy. My companion would say, 'And now my companion would like to say something' and then he would sit there and wait and not say one more word until I said something first. Sometimes he waited for a long time, and the people we were teaching felt uncomfortable, but I finally opened my mouth. That changed my mission. I learned that confidence is not a matter of personality. It is a matter of trust. We have to trust that God is there and will help us. I had to trust that God would put words in my mind when I opened my mouth. Now when I feel a lack of confidence, I know it just means I need to trust God more."

But can we maintain that trust even when people are threatening us or when they are laughing and pointing fingers? Elder Neal A. Maxwell assured us that being pointed at shouldn't worry those who are pointed in the right direction.[42]

People certainly made fun of Joseph Smith. What about Nephi? Mormon? Moroni? People teased them, too. In Old Testament times the crowds laughed and pointed at Noah, but in the end it wasn't Noah who missed the boat. In New Testament times nonbelievers cast Stephen out and stoned him. Paul was ridiculed and reviled.

"Be not afraid, . . ." the Lord told Paul, "but speak, and hold not thy peace: For I am with thee" (Acts 18:9–10). No wonder that same apostle courageously declared, "I am not ashamed of the gospel of Christ," and, "I can do all things through Christ which strengtheneth me" (Romans 1:16; Philippians 4:13).

KEEP COMMITMENTS

Russell's middle name is Tolman after his great-grandfather who was a grain farmer in Idaho. This man had many great qualities, but perhaps one of the greatest was his integrity. For several years he ran a local grain elevator and was required to buy the crops of the other farmers. On any given day he would need hundreds of thousands of dollars, which the banker loaned to him without even asking him to sign any papers. The banker knew he was a man of his word and would pay the money back when the grain was sold.

Great-grandpa Gunnell served in the Idaho State Legislature for three terms, but when business demands became too heavy, he announced he would not seek reelection. Representatives of the opposing party came to him and said that if he would reconsider they would not even run anyone against him. They simply did not want to lose a man of his integrity.

Keeping commitments builds confidence because it allows others to trust us and depend on us and also because it helps us feel good about ourselves. The word *peace* comes from the ancient word *pax,* which means "agreement." When our actions are in agreement with our beliefs and values, when our deeds match our words, then we can feel peace.

Sadly, not everyone chooses to live with integrity and peace. But we can help them. Missionaries become discouraged when people promise to read in the Book of Mormon and then don't follow through. They promise to pray and don't. They promise to attend church and never show up.

Missionaries learn to be direct and to ask, "Will you?" instead of, "Would you like to?" They resolve doubts and concerns that may stand in the way. They remind people of the commitment often and offer assistance in keeping it. Still, some people come through and some don't.

When our efforts fall short, there are some additional pointers that can be learned from Gideon in the Book of Mormon. He was trying to "commit" King Limhi to a plan of escape (see Mosiah 22:3–4). First, he stood before the king. He talked to him face to face and not over the phone or by e-mail. Nothing is more powerful than eye contact and asking for a handshake to accompany a verbal commitment. Next, Gideon reminded the king that the king knew Gideon well and had listened to him in the past with positive results. Gideon also said, "I will be thy servant" (v. 4). In other words, "My only motive is to serve you. I have nothing to gain personally." Finally, Gideon presented a specific plan. He didn't deal in generalities but outlined some clear expectations and goals. He then highlighted the result or the blessing that would be received. After Gideon laid such careful groundwork, it is no wonder that "the king hearkened unto the words of Gideon" (v. 9).

WHAT I TRIED

As recounted earlier, Elder Jeffrey R. Holland told the missionaries, "Get out there and astonish someone!" That's not that hard for LDS young people, who already are quite astonishing. There was a groundbreaking study of American teenagers and religion conducted at the University of North Carolina at Chapel Hill and published in

2005. Of all the religious groups surveyed, Latter-day Saint youth came out best at avoiding risky behaviors, doing well in school, and having a positive attitude about the future. The multi-million-dollar study took four years to complete and included telephone interviews with over 3,000 randomly selected teens from across the United States, followed by 267 face-to-face interviews. Results showed that teens who are religiously involved fare better than those who aren't. However, LDS teens ranked first across almost every category.[43]

It is nice that researchers from outside the Church are seeing what I have seen throughout all my years of working with youth. It's nice that an unbiased source can validate President Hinckley's words when he says, "I love the youth of the Church. I have said again and again that I think we have never had a better generation than this."[44]

LDS young people become great the same way we learn to ride a bike. First we have to observe someone ride to see how it is done. Then the rider brings us along while we sit on the handlebars. Next come the training wheels. Then we take our place in the driver's seat and pedal while someone runs beside us. Then we have to ride enough by ourselves that we get the wobbles out.

I consider all the things I know and do that were once beyond me. When I began my mission, I was sure I would never know Spanish. Now I do. There are other things, such as playing the piano and playing basketball, things I'm still not skilled at doing. I guess I never did them enough to get the wobbles out. When it comes to fixing a car or computer I am right at the beginning. In fact, I wouldn't even know where to begin.

Why did I give up on piano and basketball when I was younger, but not on Spanish? Perhaps it comes down to the amount of success I felt (or didn't feel). When bowling, children who never knock down any pins are not going to keep bowling. No one wants to throw gutter balls all day. But when we bring in the bumper pads the inexperienced bowler tastes enough success that he is willing to keep going.

That's what Debi and I have tried to do with our children. We tried to provide the training wheels and bumper pads. Sometimes it worked. Sometimes it didn't. When we couldn't help them ourselves, we tried to find someone else who could. Elder Wayne S. Peterson of the Seventy is fond of saying, "Competence equals confidence." And it is true. But what builds competence? Until we have it ourselves, confidence comes from knowing someone is there running along behind the bike until we can take off on our own. Until we can function independently, confidence comes from knowing where to turn for assistance. What children can't do alone, they can do with help. And what they can do with help today, they can do independently—and competently—tomorrow.

RUSSELL'S RESPONSE

When Nephi and his family arrived in the promised land, they pitched their tents and planted *all* the seeds they had brought with them (see 1 Nephi 18:23–24). Not knowing the soil, climate, or patterns of rainfall, one would think that Nephi might have been cautious and planted only a few to start. Perhaps he could have watched how things would go before jumping in and planting all their precious seeds. After all, they couldn't turn around and go back for more if these didn't grow. But the scriptures record no hesitation. He showed no fear—only faith. He held nothing back, and the seeds "did grow exceedingly" and the people "were blessed in abundance" (v. 24). What gave Nephi that kind of confidence? Just read the previous seventeen-chapters' worth of experiences that taught him such unwavering faith.

Similarly, my confidence grew over time in the mission field. The same "for, with, and by" pattern we have used in this book is the pattern I have seen in my life. Like Dad says, there were many things that my parents did for me and with me until I could do them alone—like mowing the lawn, for example. Of course, now I have kindly and generously passed that wonderful opportunity along to my younger sister!

When it came to learning missionary work, I watched my parents, participated with them, and finally did it on my own. One time I remember watching was when our family lived in New Zealand and got to go white-water rafting. Upon arriving at a calm spot in the river, the guide began telling crude jokes. When she didn't get the response she expected, she said, "Don't tell me you guys are religious!"

Dad said, "More religious than you'll ever know."

She said, "I could never be religious. I like the excitement of the river too much."

Dad responded, "If you think the river is exciting, try getting to know the One who created it!"

She laughed and began asking some questions, which Dad answered. As I listened, I half expected my dad to challenge the guide to baptism right there in the river. Believe me, I was not volunteering to be one of the witnesses. In fact, I was somewhat embarrassed that the topic of religion had come up even on a river run. I wanted to hide my head in my life jacket because my father was being so bold. However, looking back, I realize that I was learning how missionary work is done.

The first time I remember participating in a missionary effort was when our family became friends with a young Korean family while the father of the family was earning an advanced degree at BYU. They were not LDS, but loved the family values taught by the Church. We invited them to our home many times. They even accompanied us to church meetings and listened to the missionaries. That was the first time I remember having the full-time missionaries in our home for more than a meal. I played with the children of the family on the trampoline, learned some Korean words, and sat by the family when they came to church. They never joined while they were in Provo, but we made sure they were contacted by the missionaries when they returned to Korea and stayed in touch by e-mail. I was learning how missionary work is done.

While I was serving my mission in Spain, President Harold G. Hillam, who previously served as president of the Europe West Area, came to speak to the missionaries. He pounded his fist on a table and said, "Preach a strong gospel!"

My companion and I returned from that conference ready to convert the world. Without even stopping at our apartment, we began knocking on doors. A man opened and, while shaking his finger at us, began the all-too-familiar response: "*Soy Católico Apostólico Romano*" ("I'm a strict Roman Catholic"). We heard these words so many times in Spain that we could finish the phrase before they could.

As the man began to close the door, President Hillam's words came to my mind: *Preach a strong gospel!* I said, "Excuse me, sir. We are representatives of Jesus Christ. If you reject us it is the same as rejecting him." I don't know if he believed me, but he did set up a return appointment.

On another occasion we entered the small store of a professional woman we'd been teaching for a while. As we sat down she began complaining about all the bad things God was sending her way. We listened to her list of struggles with her business and family. Finally she said, "I might as well turn to lying, robbing, and cheating like everyone else since God obviously is sending me no help."

My companion calmly asked if she had read the chapter we assigned her in the Book of Mormon and if she had prayed. She replied, "And how do you expect me to find time for that with everything else going on in my life?"

Once again, President Hillam's words came to my mind: *Preach a strong gospel!* I looked at this woman right in the eyes and said, "You asked God to send help and he did. He sent us. God has not abandoned you. He is reaching out to you with solutions for all your problems, but you have not done one thing we have asked. We have promised you blessings in your business and marriage if you will just read and pray. We have invited you to church and promised you greater peace and good friends. You have never come. We have discussed baptism and promised you a remission of your sins and the chance to have the constant companionship of the Holy Ghost, but you have done nothing to reach that goal."

I expected her to kick us out of her store and throw the Book of Mormon at us as we left. Instead, she actually thanked me for being so direct. She said she felt good when we came and that she would try harder. She even asked for another copy of the Book of Mormon she could give to her son. I was doing missionary work.

KEYS FOR ACTION

What Can We Do FOR Young People?

In preparing our young people to serve missions, we need to communicate high expectations. It is no surprise that excellent teachers, coaches, and leaders most often get exactly what they ask for. Many of our youth are willing to respond when challenged to stretch and give their best efforts—especially when those expectations are given with sincere and genuine concern and love.

A man once interviewed me and said, "I don't understand how you Mormons do it. You get the youth in your church to wake up early and go to religious classes. You get them to devote years on missions and pay for it themselves. You get them to live without smoking, drugs, and free sex in a world where such things are commonplace. My church couldn't get kids to do those things if they paid them."

Based on years of observing our youth, my response was, "Mormon young people know what is expected and that it doesn't just come from the Church but from the Lord."

Many young people thrive on meeting those high expectations. Still, there are some who become discouraged because they feel as though they have to be perfect. As important as it is to communicate high expectations, we must make sure those expectations are also realistic. Expecting a young man to serve a mission is a high but realistic expectation. Telling him, as one father did, "You better get called to Japan. They always send the smart ones to Japan," creates an unrealistic (and inaccurate) perception. Such expressions overwhelm young people.

What Can We Do WITH Young People?

We can help teens confront their fears. A mother told about a time when her son was asked to speak in stake conference. "He was terrified," she said. "He doesn't think of himself as much of a public speaker, and he hates big crowds. He is much happier being with animals than people."

As the big day drew closer, the mother recognized all the signs of stress. In fact, these weren't just signs, they were massive electronic billboards. She tried to help. She was willing to listen, but he was in no mood to talk.

Finally, on the day before the conference, she tapped on his bedroom door. He said, "Come in." She entered to find him surrounded by scriptures, church books, and wadded-up sheets of paper. His tenseness and nervousness were obvious. She asked, "Look, what's the worst thing that could happen?"

"I'll make an idiot of myself."

"So, what can we do to avoid that?" Her tone showed confidence in his ability to cope. She was treating his fear with respect.

"Well, would you listen to what I've written so far?"

She was surprised at the request. If she had suggested the same thing, he probably would have told her to get lost. She listened intently, praised him generously, and offered a few suggestions.

The following day the young man gave an excellent talk. His mother said, "It was short, but wonderful. He spoke sincerely of his love for the Savior. The visiting authority even commented on how well he did, which made him feel on top of the world. I was really relieved and happy that it turned out as a good experience."

Once "the worst thing that could happen" is out in the open, it can be demystified. Panic and fear become less intense. When young people honestly define their fears, they can confront them. The problem isn't automatically solved, but the sting has been taken away.

What Can Young People Do BY THEMSELVES?

Be yourself. The objective is for missionaries to be natural and let their own personalities shine when interacting with people. One missionary wrote to me, "On my mission I've learned to be myself. I've found the best way to reach people is by just being me and not putting on any fronts or following any scripts." He's correct. The most successful missionaries are often those who relate easily to people, show a sincere interest, maintain their sense of humor, and find it easy to express their love for people and for the gospel. If we feel as though we have to leave our personalities behind when we check in to the MTC, we're going to have long missions. In Doctrine and Covenants 4 we read that we must serve with all our heart, might, mind, and strength. That includes serving with our unique personalities as well.

Sometimes people use the phrase "It's just the way I am" as an excuse for being mean, undisciplined, lazy, or crude. That's not appropriate for those of us who understand the eternal nature of our existence. When we talk of being ourselves, it must be our eternal selves, our best selves. To say, "I'm just being me" does not release us from our responsibility to repent, refine ourselves, and become more like the Savior. On the contrary, it allows us to believe that—

amazingly—we actually have that potential within. Such a belief gives us the courage to share our unique gifts.

One elder in our mission, for example, was an incredible guitarist. He used his musical talents as a way of creating an interest in his message. Sometimes he played for a few and other times for hundreds, but the point is he played as only he could.

What if an elder excels at swimming, rock climbing, or other activities that can't be done on a mission? Even if the activity itself needs to be put on hold, there is nothing preventing that missionary from transferring the lessons learned in the development of that talent into missionary service. The determination swimmers and rock climbers have learned is a useful thing in missionary life, and the experiences they have had in the pool or on the cliff can often be used as examples in the lessons they teach.

The approach to teaching in *Preach My Gospel* frees missionaries to use their own words and examples from their own lives. Investigators' hearts are often touched to the core as one missionary shares the struggles of his handicapped brother and another shares his own struggle learning to read. Using the scriptures to teach a concept is vital, but we can also explain how that concept or scripture became meaningful to us. Testimonies must be borne, but occasionally we need to tell the stories behind how those testimonies were gained.

In an object lesson at a zone conference, a missionary held up a pineapple and said that people are a lot like pineapples. They are rough and prickly on the outside, but soft and sweet on the inside. He then took a knife and cut away the outside of the pineapple saying, "Our personal experience is the tool that will get us through to the hearts of those we are trying to teach and reach."

It has been my experience that people relate better to missionaries who are "real." It is our unique personalities and talents along with our personal experiences that constitute who we are.

Remember, when God calls us on a mission, that includes all the positive and negative experiences that have gone into shaping us. They come with us. Missionaries are not expected to be cardboard cutouts or carbon copies of the actors in the Church training films. We are expected to be ourselves.

Fear comes from feeling as though you have to fit into a mold. Confidence comes from knowing that you just have to be yourself. As one missionary put it, "Hey, I can do that! In fact, I can be myself better than anyone else can!"

10

▲ ▲ ▲

GOING THE EXTRA SMILE

Most people have received more than enough lessons on keeping a positive attitude. We have all been advised to view the glass as half full instead of half empty, turn life's lemons into lemonade, and count blessings rather than problems. We've all heard it takes more muscles to frown than to smile, and we've read the classic poem about the two men who looked out through prison bars—one seeing mud while the other sees stars. Such sayings serve as good reminders, but if not kept in perspective, they can actually be discouraging. After all, some days we relate more to the man who saw mud. The picture of a prisoner blissfully stargazing from his cell definitely represents a positive ideal, but on some days it seems unrealistic and unattainable.

We're human. Everyone experiences a range of moods, including negative emotions. That's not necessarily bad. It's okay to occasionally feel down and discouraged. Of course we must learn to take responsibility for our feelings and do our best to stay positive, but now and then who cares whether the dumb glass is half anything and we don't even want lemonade! The fact that we all sometimes feel that way is why we laugh when we see a bumper sticker that says, "Smile first thing in the morning (and get it over with)," or, "Want to wake up with a smile? Sleep with a hanger in your mouth!"

Russell loved Dr. Seuss books when he was younger. One of his favorites is the last complete book Dr. Seuss wrote called *My Many Colored Days.*[45] It tells about the variety of moods or colors that filled Dr. Seuss's life. He wrote about how sometimes he felt red, blue, green, and so on. Dr. Seuss never even got to illustrate his book before he passed away, but it was still published—an insightful parting message from a beloved author.

For missionaries, keeping a positive attitude doesn't mean we have to suppress the dark colors. It simply means we must learn to bring the light and dark colors of our lives together in balance, harmony, and perspective. It means we learn how to put our moods and concerns on the back burner and the needs of others up front. Regardless of the current color of their day, missionaries can make a sincere effort to smile more, smile first, and smile despite problems.

SMILE MORE

My father and Russell's grandfather, Ray T. Wilcox, served his first mission in Tahiti, so we have heard many stories of the faithful and wonderful Saints living in the islands of French Polynesia. When our family had the opportunity to visit Tahiti, we were impressed with how multilingual the people were. Most spoke French and Tahitian fluently. Many spoke English as well. However, the thing that impressed us most of all was how fluent the Tahitians were in the most important language. Grandma Wilcox calls it the language of smile.

When Debi and I attended the temple in Tahiti, we were impressed by how people smiled and extended their hands (and not just the temple workers). As we completed the endowment session and entered the celestial room, it was easy to feel as though we were in heaven—encircled by love and warmed by acceptance, literally surrounded by smiles.

As we consciously attempt to smile more, we can help others feel the way Debi and I felt in the Papeete Tahiti Temple. We don't have to be in a celestial room to act in a celestial way. We don't have to be on a South Pacific island to give others a taste of paradise. We all know how to speak the language of smile. We just need to do it a little more.

When people go to Disneyland, they expect to see a happy Mickey Mouse. It may be the last hour of his shift, but Mickey Mouse can't let up. He may have met hundreds of children throughout the day, but this could very well be the next child's first and perhaps only encounter with the famous mouse.

In the same way, people expect missionaries to be happy and outgoing. Missionaries may have knocked on hundreds of doors, but it may be the first meeting for the one opening the next door. Missionaries may be tired and want to relax on the bus ride home, but like Mickey Mouse, they have an image to keep up. They need to be the ones who make eye contact, greet others with a smile, pay a sincere compliment, and try to begin a friendly conversation. Sunday may be the end of a long and exhausting week, but members don't come to church expecting to buoy up a missionary. They expect "Mickey" to be there welcoming them and giving them encouragement to keep going.

As Russell teaches at the MTC, he has noticed that many new missionaries become so preoccupied with practicing Spanish, lessons, and scriptures that they sometimes forget to practice smiling. They speak, teach, recite scriptures, and testify without ever smiling. He sometimes shares with them the scripture found in 2 Nephi 9:39, which reads, "To be spiritually-minded is life eternal." Then he points out that the first letters of the words starting with *spiritually* spell s-m-i-l-e: **S**piritually **M**inded **I**s **L**ife **E**ternal. Indeed, to be spiritual doesn't mean we have to be serious and solemn all the time. We can enjoy the moment and smile. Russell tells the missionaries that unless they smile, people are not even going to be interested in the language, lessons, and scriptures they are working so hard to learn.

Elder Joe J. Christensen, former member of the Presidency of the Seventy and also a former president of the MTC in Provo, said, "Smile. Force it if you have to. . . . Your level of spirituality is also directly related to how well you fill the Lord's commandments to 'be of good cheer' and 'lift up your heart and rejoice.' For us to be of good cheer is a commandment and not merely a suggestion."[46]

SMILE FIRST

It is not uncommon to hear stories of people who have been offended at church because "no one even smiled or said hello." The question we always have is how many people did *they* greet? How many people did *they* smile at? Still, they don't see that as their responsibility.

Too often we wait for someone else to smile before we smile back. We wait for another person to nod or wave before we do the same. Are we puppets who can only respond when someone pulls the right string? Or are we willing to initiate positive interactions?

A young woman once said her goal was "to be a thermostat and not a thermometer." When asked what she meant, she explained, "A thermometer measures the temperature. A thermostat sets it. Anyone can measure the temperature, but I want to be the one who sets it." And nothing sets the right temperature like smiling first.

As we walk across campus at Brigham Young University, we try to smile and say hello to those we pass, whether or not we know them. Often when I am walking toward people on a sidewalk I will encounter people who try to avoid contact by averting their eyes and looking down. I don't let them get away with that. I usually lean right over, catch their eye, and say a loud, "Hi!" People generally respond with a laugh as they realize how silly it is that sidewalks often get more attention than the people who walk on them. Russell gets frustrated when he casually says hi to girls on campus, and they quickly show him their wedding rings. What? Married women can't say hi as they pass someone on a sidewalk? Sometimes we greet people and no one even notices because they are listening to their iPods or talking on cell phones. Still, we don't let that stop us.

Artist James C. Christensen once asked President Spencer W. Kimball, "President, if you were going to hang a painting of the Savior in your office, what would you want that picture to be like?"

President Kimball took off his glasses and got very close to Brother Christensen's face. Then he said, "Can you see anything in my eyes that tells you that I love people? In that picture, I would like to see in the Savior's eyes that he truly loves people. It is not affected; it is not his job. He truly loves all people."[47]

A smile doesn't just communicate happiness—it communicates love. It's easy to smile first when our hearts are filled with love. Then, like President Kimball explained, it is not our "job." It is our nature. Perhaps putting a smile on our faces is a huge step toward having Christ's image in our countenances.

SMILE DESPITE

Our family was impressed with the positive attitude shown by our former neighbor Ron Zaret, who said, "The bad news is that I have to have another back surgery, but the good news is they are waiting until after my kidney surgery." How's that for smiling despite problems? Later he told us, "The bad news is they ended up removing one of my kidneys because it was full of cancer. The good news is now I only have one kidney left to produce kidney stones." Can you imagine how such an attitude endears Brother Zaret to those who are lucky enough to know him?

Following Brother Zaret's line of thinking, I guess the bad news is that life is full of disappointments, trials, sadness, injustice, and pain. The good news is that we have the power to smile despite it all.

Happiness is a choice and not just a mood. Jesus said, "Blessed are ye that weep now: for ye shall laugh" (Luke 6:21).

One missionary said, "On my mission I have learned to find my smile and be happy. It hasn't been easy because my happiness was always linked to success and achievements, and on the mission sometimes those don't come the way you would like. I have had to learn to be happy even when others make poor choices."

One mother struggled when her teenage daughter became defiant and belligerent and began breaking the Word of Wisdom and the law of chastity. The girl fought against authority and eventually dropped out of high school. The mother said, "This was as difficult a challenge as any I had previously faced. I became despondent and inconsolable." She fasted, prayed, and sought advice from her bishop. She asked for priesthood blessings and spent hours reading scriptures and books on dealing with difficult teenagers. Still, she was miserable. She said, "I wondered, *Where is the joy in family life? When will these problems cease?*" Finding no resolution, she lost all confidence in her ability to parent. She felt desperate, angry, and helpless.

The next few years were difficult for this mother, but slowly she began to realize that though there were things about her daughter's life over which she had little control, there were things about her own life that she could change. She said, "I decided I needed to go back to the basics of the gospel and build a stronger, more solid spirituality. I wondered when was the last time, for instance, I had offered prayers of gratitude. Had I completely forgotten my many blessings? Had I actively looked for the good qualities of my struggling daughter? Did I appreciate the obedient members of my family, or had I forgotten their faithfulness?"

This mother tried to fill herself with good and positive thoughts. She read uplifting books and diligently followed a personal exercise program. Instead of listening to the radio while in the car, she read the scriptures in the morning and pondered them while driving. Did the daughter see the error of her ways? Did she turn around, repent, and gain a testimony? Actually, she did make some progress but has not yet returned to full activity in the Church. But that's not the point. Did the mother learn to smile despite her daughter's poor choices? Yes.[48]

Another example of smiling despite problems happened when our family lived in New Zealand, where I was directing a study-abroad program for Brigham Young University. It was on the world-changing day of September 11, 2001 (actually, because of the time difference, it was September 12 for us) when terrorists committed their vicious crimes. A friend in our ward in Auckland called around 3:00 A.M. and told us the United States was under attack. Debi took the call, and when she came back to bed and reported, I was sure it was a joke. Still, who would joke about something like that? Debi and I got up, went downstairs, switched on the television quietly so as to not awaken the children, and then watched along with the rest of the world as the unthinkable horror unfolded. Like everyone else, we were stunned and shocked. We prayed and didn't try to hold back our tears. Russell woke up for early-morning seminary and was surprised to see his parents watching TV. We explained what was happening, but it didn't really hit Russell how serious it was until he was at seminary and listened to the comments and sympathetic condolences of his teacher and fellow students. I had to call each of the study-abroad students with the news and instructions I had received from BYU after the attacks.

The students were instructed to go about their regular schedules, which meant reporting to their assigned classrooms where they were student-teaching. Then, one at a time, the calls started coming from the schools. They couldn't do it, not that day. Russell and I drove around Auckland, picking up the students from the schools and bringing them to our home, where they all sat watching the news and grieving together. The group was half a world away from all that was happening, but we felt the devastation as if we were right there.

How does one smile at a time like that? The anger, pain, fear, and vulnerability we all felt were emotions that were real and intense. In that moment smiles were hard to come by, but over the weeks and months that followed, they came—not smiles because of what had occurred but smiles because of what we know that helped us keep things in perspective. We know about the plan of salvation and the gift of agency. We know God is all-powerful. He could have stopped it all at any moment, but faith is not just knowing God can. Faith is also understanding why sometimes he doesn't. Along with being all-powerful, God is also all-knowing (see Moroni 7:22). We can trust him because he sees the end from the beginning and has a plan for our lives.

How did we make it through that experience? It helped to hear a prophet speak about the reality of the spirit world, resurrection, and the Atonement. It helped to know that, though it never justifies it, good can come from evil and peace can be felt amid conflict.

In times of discouragement it is not cute sayings about the glass being half full or looking for silver linings that give us strength to carry on. It is knowing the gospel and keeping covenants that provides the will and power to survive. Elder Robert E. Wells of the First Quorum of the Seventy has assured us, "In spite of all the problems in the world today, peace can come to the hearts of each of us as we follow the Savior."[49]

As we face tragedy, whether it is witnessed by billions around the world or is so personal and private that no one is aware of it but God, we can take solace in the Savior's words: "Fear not, little children, for you are mine, and I have overcome the world" (D&C 50:41). It is in that knowledge that we find the strength to go the extra smile—smile more, smile first, and smile despite anything that comes.

WHAT I TRIED

When I returned from serving as mission president, many asked, "What should we do to help our children better prepare?" My answer wasn't what people expected to hear: "Turn off the TV a little more. Turn off the Nintendo and computer games." What missionaries need are people skills, and those are not developed or honed in front of a monitor. Young people are always quick to point out that Nintendo is good for hand-eye coordination. Sorry, but that is not a skill that is very useful on a mission. What *does* make a big difference are people skills. We need to be able to shake hands and look people in their eyes. That's the hand-eye coordination that counts. Missionaries spend time studying and teaching, but they also spend time meeting people, visiting with people, listening to people, and learning to love people.

We have tried to prepare our children for that by limiting TV viewing—we have not thrown out the TV altogether, but you won't see it on a lot at our house. Our goal is not to watch *Friends,* our goal is to *have* friends. With the TV off it is amazing how much time there is for more productive efforts—including more social interactions.

Three activities that give us a chance to visit are eating meals together, playing games, and doing puzzles. One young convert once came to our house when we were eating dinner and was surprised we had the TV off. He said that his family watched as they ate. He was also surprised that we ate together in the same place. He said that they usually filled their plates and retreated to their own bedrooms where they each had a TV and could watch whatever they wanted. His comments broke my heart as I thought of the interactions we have enjoyed through the years during meal times that he had missed out on.

I'm making it sound as though we all sit around a formally set dining table during meals, discussing politics or gospel doctrine. I'm afraid not. Usually, we just sit at the kitchen counter, but we sit there together. Usually, we get to talking about what has been going on during the day or what is coming up the next day, but we are speaking, listening, and making eye contact with each other.

My wife plays Ping-Pong with the kids. I gave up because I spent the whole time chasing balls around, but Debi can actually hit them and so it gives her a chance to talk with the kids and let them talk to her. I get a similar opportunity when we play other games. It really doesn't matter which one—we have gone through a lot of them through the years. It's not that I'm a nut about Rook, but I do like the conversation and joking that accompany a good game.

When the children were young we used to put a jigsaw puzzle out during general conference if we were viewing it at home. It was our attempt to keep them in the room where they could hear the talks. After working so hard to complete a puzzle, we couldn't bear to put it back in the box, so Debi started gluing them together and hanging them in the garage. Now the montage covers two entire walls. That's a lot of general conference sessions! At this point, the children are older and we don't do puzzles to keep them busy and quiet during conference sessions. Rather, now we enjoy solving puzzles at times other than general conference so that we are all seated around the same table at the same time. What we once did to keep kids quiet now promotes a lot of talking.

Everyone keeps telling me that e-mail, iPods, cell phones, and text messaging are bringing the world together, but all I see is more people who are living more isolated lives than ever. It's great that we can talk to friends whenever we want, but when do we learn to talk to the people next to us and make new friends? My daughter Wendee gets frustrated when she's with people who spend their whole time together texting others. She asks, "Why don't they talk to me when I'm right there?"

RUSSELL'S RESPONSE

My dad always swore we would never have a Nintendo, but when I was a little kid I couldn't understand his reasoning. I was in first grade and figured that if my dad wasn't going to get me a Nintendo I would have to take my appeal to Santa. I wrote letters and even asked my mom if we could visit Santa when he came to a local store. Santa asked me what I wanted, and I said, "A Nintendo." He winked at my mom and said, "You'll have to be really good." I didn't know my parents were discussing my wish behind my back, but Dad was doing his own letter writing to Santa, telling him we would pass on the Nintendo. As a sixth-grade teacher, Dad had seen too many boys who were great at playing Nintendo and poor at reading, and he didn't want that happening to me. I didn't know that. All I knew was that Santa told me that if I was good, the Nintendo was mine. Finally, on Christmas Eve day I told my mom that I just knew I would get a Nintendo because I had been the best boy in the world. What's a mother to do? Sometimes Santa needs a little help. She went right out as the stores were closing and got the very last one—without telling my dad.

The next morning we were opening gifts, and you can only imagine my delight as I opened a brand-new Nintendo. You can also imagine how wide my father's eyes became and how sweetly my mom said, "Why, wasn't that nice of Santa?"

Looking back, I don't think the game was abused. My parents made sure of that. Actually, it was a lot of fun and gave me a way to make friends and talk with other kids (and I still learned to read). So, even though I know my dad isn't too big on those kinds of games, I think they can have a place. The point is not to let them consume all your time or get in the way of building relationships.

The same is true for cell phones. When I first got home from my mission I was excited to get my own cell phone. It seemed like everyone had one, and I couldn't wait to join in.

On the same day that I finally got my long-awaited cell phone, our neighborhood had a yard sale (which wasn't much of a sale for us because my mom kept giving everything away for free). As I played on my new cell phone and became acquainted with all its features I noticed a lady looking at some of the items. I was tempted to just keep exploring the phone but instead put it away and began talking with her. I found out she was from Argentina and, having served in Spain, I began to speak with her in Spanish. She was not a member of the Church but had attended meetings with her husband a few times. I was able to get her phone number as a reference for the missionaries.

After talking to my new friend I felt so happy and grateful that I'd started speaking to her. I'd been excited to get a cell phone, but in the end found it a lot less exciting than meeting new people and sharing the gospel.

When I was younger there were two things that always used to bug me about going places with my dad: 1) he would always pick up litter (actually, he was smart and would tell me it was a game or race so I would do it with him.), and 2) he would always say hi to everyone. Now I am turning into my dad! If a loose paper ever falls out of my pocket, I have to turn around and pick it up, and I try to say hi to people, too.

While I was growing up, my mom worked part-time as a nurse in the same-day surgery unit at the local hospital. I always looked forward to picking her up from work because it meant I could get a treat from the vending machine. My snack break was always accompanied by one of the other nurses telling me what a great nurse my mom was. As I grew older I realized it was not because she knew all the answers or could put in an IV perfectly (in fact, she always wanted to practice on me!). The reason the other nurses called my mom a good nurse was that she cared so much about the patients and their families. She was friendly, sensitive, and empathetic. Sure, she had to know her stuff, but it was her caring and kindness that people appreciated most.

A saying we heard a lot in my mission was, "We are people teaching investigators, not robots teaching lessons." That perspective helped us keep the right focus. A scripture we heard quoted often was Doctrine and Covenants 84:85: "Treasure up in your minds continually the words of life." I have gained much from treasuring up the scriptures and words of the living prophets. However, as I consider how much I value the relationships made in my mission, I think that maybe the words of life we can choose to treasure up are found not just in the scriptures, but also in our everyday interactions.

KEYS TO ACTION

What Can We Do FOR Young People?

Offer sincere compliments. Mother Teresa said, "Kind words can be short and easy to speak, but their echoes are truly endless."[50] Debi has never forgotten an occasion in her teenage years when someone told her that in a meeting, a leader had complimented Debi on her dependability. While the leader didn't say the words directly to Debi, she learned about them, and they made a positive difference in how she felt about herself.

In our family home evenings, we have traditionally begun by reciting our family motto: Mosiah 4:15—"Teach them to love one another, and to serve one another." Sometimes we recite some of the Articles of Faith, too, and if we are not in a fight by then about which ones to recite or whether or not to sing them, then we usually give each other compliments. When the children were younger they always said the same thing over and over ("Mom, you sure made a good dinner!"). But as they grew, the diversity of the compliments improved and so did their ability to receive them graciously.

You would think that now that the children are older, we would have outgrown the practice. But does anyone ever outgrow the need to be noticed, appreciated, and valued? I think we need our little compliment time now more than ever.

What Can We Do WITH Young People?

There are three things we can do with young people to help them develop better social skills. First, we can create social environments for them. Initiate gatherings with family and friends. Invite a family from the ward over to share a family home evening or game night. Invite neighbors and investigators over for dinner. Try arranging the seating so that young people don't miss out on the conversation.

Second, when children receive a speaking assignment in Primary or sacrament meeting, practice with them to make sure it is a positive experience. Teach them how to look up and make eye contact rather than just read their talks. Help them share a personal experience along with a scripture or story. One public school teacher in California was always impressed with the confidence of the LDS children in his classroom. He said, "Most were never afraid to get up and talk before the class. They spoke up and shared opinions when others were too timid." That good impression actually led him to investigate and join the Church. Obviously, our children have more opportunities to speak before groups than some other children. Still, with just a little bit more preparation and effort, we can take greater advantage of those opportunities and help our children communicate even more effectively.

Third, encourage working in service-oriented jobs. One former mission president made the comment that young people who had worked in service-oriented jobs to earn money for their mission gained more than money. They actually came better prepared for missionary service because they were used to dealing with the public and serving people.

What Can Young People Do BY THEMSELVES?

Work on making a good first impression and initiating conversations. Make eye contact with people, smile, greet them with "Hello," "Good Morning," or, "It's a pleasure to meet you." Just notice those around you. You can pay a compliment ("You have a beautiful family") or make an appropriate friendly comment ("My mom loves dogs, too").

You can also ask questions. When waiting in the check-out line at the grocery store behind a mother with children, just say, "How old are your kids?" When you're pumping gas next to someone, ask, "Where are you from?" If the other person doesn't want to talk, let the conversation die. However, if he or she answers with some interest, keep talking.

Sometimes the Church comes up naturally (he says, "Oh, you're from Utah. Are you Mormon?" or you say, "You're from _____? I have a friend who served a mission there"). If the gospel doesn't come up, don't worry about it. Just talk. Show interest in someone else.

President Scott G. Waldram, who served as the president of the DR Congo Kinshasa Mission in Africa, says that salesmen in stores always get further with him by asking, "How are you?" rather than, "May I help you?" He likes it if they show interest in him as a person and not just as a potential customer. It is the difference between selling and caring. It may seem awkward at first, but it gets easier the more you try. Elderly people are usually a good place to start, or talk to children when they are with their parents. It doesn't really matter who—just challenge yourself to speak up.

Elder Russell Osguthorpe, who served as president of the South Dakota Rapid City Mission, taught a missionary preparation class at BYU when he first returned home. One of the homework assignments for the course was simply to talk to people. Students were to strike up a conversation with someone they didn't know and then report back. When the course was being evaluated, most students said that of all the assignments given, the most valuable was having to get outside their comfort zones and talk to people they didn't know.

One missionary who served in Chile said, "I didn't ever have a lot of contact with people before the mission and now I love it. I love the human contact and relationships I form. I see how they give meaning to life. Before, I just existed in my own world. I never wanted to talk to anyone. I didn't see the point. But now I want to talk to everyone because I love getting to know people and seeing them change. It is my greatest satisfaction."

Conclusion

▲ ▲ ▲

TODAY, IN TWENTY YEARS, AND FOREVER

It was President James E. Faust who called Debi and me to serve as mission president and companion. President Faust had recently given a talk in general conference about the famous children's story *The Little Engine That Could,* so when he asked me, "Can you handle being a mission president in a Spanish-speaking mission?" I answered, "I think I can. I think I can." It made President Faust laugh.

Our interview was one of many similar interviews done each year by President Faust, but it will always be a special memory for Debi and me. Among other things, President Faust told us that our effectiveness would not be measured just by the number of baptisms but also by where our missionaries would be in twenty years. Though President Faust has doubtless shared the same insight with many mission presidents, I took the words personally. The motto for our mission became: *Hoy, en veinte años, y para siempre jamas*—"Today, in twenty years, and forever." I hoped it would help the missionaries see that the goal is not just to be strong and active today, but to remain so for twenty years and beyond.

One of the saddest things I observe is a returned missionary whose dress and demeanor show no evidence that he has served a mission. My heart goes out to him, and I pray that he will remember who he is and live accordingly. When Russell left home for the first time to attend college, as his parents we hoped he would room with a returned missionary, and we were a little worried when all the roommates turned out to be eighteen-year-olds. When Russell called to inform me that the final roommate who came was an RM, I was grateful and relieved, but that feeling didn't last. It turned out the RM was the only one in the apartment who didn't read his scriptures regularly and who woke up "sick" on too many Sundays. While the others attended church, the RM often sat at home playing computer games. His behavior and the example he was providing were disappointing, to say nothing of the loss of the Spirit in his own life.

On the other hand, we have all seen the wonderful example of a returned missionary who remains faithful, going to the temple and faithfully attending to his priesthood responsibilities, despite his busy school, social, and work schedule. What's the difference? Did one RM have it hard while the other had it easy? No. The truth is that both faced the same awkward transition home. Both faced temptations and difficult choices. Both had to balance various aspects of their lives. Both received support from others—sometimes too much and sometimes too little. "Easy" and "hard" were not two separate bicycles they were handed. Rather, "easy" and "hard" are two wheels on the same bike. Where those missionaries end up in twenty years will not be determined by the wheels but by how they steer. They can choose to go downhill or turn toward the mountain and say, "I think I can. I think I can."

Consider these thoughts from returned missionaries who have stayed strong:

An elder: "Just when you figure out how to be a good missionary and how to help people commit and make changes, it's time to go home. The work would go better if they started calling returned missionaries on second missions. Of course, I guess—in a way—that's what they already do."

A wonderful sister missionary: "The mission is just an MTC for life."

Another sister: "A mission is a way of life and not a period in your life. It's an attitude, not an act."

An elder: "It was a hard adjustment to come home. I missed the mission. Things hadn't changed much at home, but I had changed. My nonmember friend took me to a comedy club to see my favorite comic from before the mission. I didn't laugh once all night. I couldn't believe I used to think he was funny. He was just negative, mean, and crude. How had I changed so much? It was all the small things I was doing in the mission. I decided that if I wanted to feel like I did in the mission I'd better keep doing the small things I did in the mission."

Another elder: "When I got home I don't think anyone noticed I had changed. They all thought of me as a good Mormon kid before I left and now they saw me the same way. What they didn't know is that I finally became what they always assumed I was."

An elder: "After serving a mission, I understand at least a little about what the Savior must have felt when everyone rejected him. It didn't make me mad or frustrated as much as it made me just plain sad. I was sad these people didn't know what they were doing. I was sad they chose to walk blindly through life with no concern for the future. I was sad that getting drunk every weekend seemed to be their only purpose. What a waste. I never want God or Jesus to feel that way about me."

A grateful sister missionary: "I am just praying that if I lose my memory one day, I won't forget this mission. I don't want to ever forget what I felt and did, what I taught and the people I loved, what I learned and the joy I felt. If I ever begin to slip, that memory will keep me strong. When we take the sacrament we promise to remember Christ always. I think remembering my mission will help me remember him."

A wise sister: "I don't want the gospel to just be part of my life. I want it to be part of me."

Some returned missionaries struggle and others stay strong, but what about the ones in the middle? One young man arrived home determined not to slip. He set high goals and kept studying and praying as he had on the mission. However, as time went on, he became busy with other things and made new friends. Slowly, he fell into some lazy habits that brought him down. He let his temple recommend expire and made no effort to renew it. He did not attend church regularly or serve in a calling. He bounced between the singles ward in his home stake and a local student ward without becoming a part of either. He made no effort to share the gospel with others or complete his home teaching. Tithing and fast offerings were hit-and-miss. When his mission president contacted him and asked how he was doing, he described himself as "just coasting" and "taking a break."

The young man was obviously embarrassed to confess his behavior to his mission president and tried to justify his poor choices by saying, "President, I'm still a good person. I'm still trying to be nice and live a Christ-like life."

Is that how he was defining *Christ-like?* Jesus was certainly good and nice, but was that all? Jesus got baptized and kept his covenants. He observed the Sabbath and obeyed the other commandments. He prayed often, resisted temptation, valued the temple, and in all things built the kingdom and did the will of his Father. Could this returned missionary really describe himself as Christ-like?

Joseph Fielding McConkie wrote:

> The true disciple cannot say to God, "I will be your disciple but without chastity," or "I will consecrate myself but leave my wealth intact," or "I will follow you but not your prophet," or "I will be your servant, but I will not comply with the ordinances of salvation."[51] Responsibility attends true discipleship.

The returned missionary assured his mission president, "Don't worry. It's not like I have left the Church. I'm just taking a little vacation."

His mission president said, "The only problem is that in the Church there is no such thing as vacation pay."

Elder Francisco J. Viñas of the First Quorum of the Seventy once spoke at a fireside for returned missionaries. Much effort had been made to search out and invite men and women who once served valiantly but who were now less active. Elder Viñas said to them:

> You say you have to work on Sunday and don't have time for a calling? You say you don't want to pay tithing? Well, you will probably make more money and be able to buy a nicer car, but what does that say about where your heart is? One day you will have to go to God and ask for something money can't buy. Perhaps it will be for the healing of a sick child or the life of a spouse. You will want that blessing more than anything else. Whether or not the blessing is granted, how are you going to feel in that moment going to God? How will you ask for something so big when you have done so little?

The mission president told the returned missionary about Elder Viñas's words, but the RM revealed how shallow his understanding was when he responded, "Don't worry, President. It will all work out. In the parable of the laborers in Matthew 20 the one who comes at the end of the day gets paid just as much as the one who has worked all day."

The mission president said, "But the laborers at the end of the day did miss something. They missed the labor. Those who came late didn't miss the pay, but they missed the work."

The young man laughed. "I don't think I'll feel too bad about missing the work. Honestly, President, don't worry about me."

But the mission president did worry. He knew that along with missing the work, the young man was missing all the learning, relationships, and memories that come with it. He would never be able to buy back the time he was wasting or recover the experiences he might have been having.

Some missionaries may be happy when their missions end. They may be glad to call it quits and leave the work to someone else. Others feel differently. As their missions end they would happily trade every blessing they might receive—all the pay at the end of the day—for just one thing: the chance to keep laboring.

For such missionaries President David O. McKay's call for every member to be a missionary comes as an answer to prayer.[52] It means that they can continue doing what they love most—the work. Their purpose doesn't change, just their plaque. Their focus doesn't change, just their routine and how they punch the clock. Their heart doesn't change, just their sectors and companions.

These are the missionaries who realize that those who choose to miss the work also miss the opportunity of working side by side with the Savior. Today, in twenty years, and forever, Christ will be working. If we would be near him—and be like him—we must also be found engaged in his work.

As mentioned, President James E. Faust told Debi and me that our success would be measured in part by where our missionaries will be twenty years down the road. Those missionaries know that their twenty-year reunion will come for them just as Russell knows it will come for him and his mission president. Will it be a time of joy as was the reunion of Alma and the sons of Mosiah (see Alma 27:16–19)? Will we all rejoice because we are still brothers and sisters in the Lord? It doesn't depend on what we did in the mission as much as it depends on what we are doing today. The bar is set for members as well as missionaries. Now we must raise ourselves to the bar—*hoy, en veinte años, y para siempre jamas.*

NOTES

1. M. Russell Ballard, "The Greatest Generation of Missionaries," *Ensign,* November 2002, 47.

2. M. Russell Ballard, "One More," *Ensign,* May 2005, 71.

3. Vaughn J. Featherstone, *A Generation of Excellence* (Salt Lake City: Bookcraft, 1975), 11.

4. Mary Brown, "I'll Go Where You Want Me to Go," in *Hymns of The Church of Jesus Christ of Latter-day Saints* (Salt Lake City: The Church of Jesus Christ of Latter-day Saints, 1985), no. 270.

5. David S. Baxter, "Faith, Service, Constancy," *Ensign,* November 2006, 14.

6. John Taylor, in *Teachings of the Presidents of the Church: John Taylor* (Salt Lake City: The Church of Jesus Christ of Latter-day Saints, 2001), 99.

7. David O. McKay, quoted in Richard N. Holzapfel and William W. Slaughter, *Prophets of the Latter Days* (Salt Lake City: Deseret Book, 2003), 119.

8. Neal A. Maxwell, *Things As They Really Are* (Salt Lake City: Deseret Book, 1978), xiv.

9. Neal A. Maxwell, *Of One Heart* (Salt Lake City: Deseret Book, 1975), 37.

10. Ezra Taft Benson, "Born of God," *Ensign,* July 1989, 2.

11. Spencer W. Kimball, "Absolute Truth," *Ensign,* September 1978, 7.

12. Kimball, "Absolute Truth," *Ensign,* September 1978, 8.

13. David A. Bednar, "Because We Have Them Before Our Eyes," *New Era,* April 2006, 2.

14. W. Grant Bangerter, "It's a Two-Way Street," *Ensign,* July 1986, 71.

15. Joseph Smith, *History of the Church of Jesus Christ of Latter-day Saints,* 7 vols., ed. B. H. Roberts, 2d. ed. rev. (Salt Lake City: The Church of Jesus Christ of Latter-day Saints, 1932–51), 1:170.

16. Dallin H. Oaks, *The Lord's Way* (Salt Lake City: Deseret Book, 1991), 56.

17. *Preach My Gospel,* 1; emphasis added. See also Book of Mormon Title Page.

18. Terryl L. Givens, *By the Hand of Mormon: The American Scripture That Launched a New World Religion* (Oxford: Oxford University Press, 2002).

19. Givens, *By the Hand of Mormon,* 40.

20. Givens, *By the Hand of Mormon,* 40.

21. Susan Easton Black, *Finding Christ through the Book of Mormon* (Salt Lake City: Deseret Book, 1987), 13.

22. *Preach My Gospel,* 104.

23. David A. Bednar, Church Educational System fireside, February 4, 2007.

24. Gordon B. Hinckley, "This Is the Work of the Master," *Ensign,* May 1995, 71.

25. See Edward L. Kimball, *Lengthen Your Stride: The Presidency of Spencer W. Kimball* (Salt Lake City: Deseret Book, 2005), 435–45.

26. Ezra Taft Benson, "Think on Christ," *Ensign,* March 1989, 4.

27. Truman G. Madsen, *Christ and the Inner Life* (Salt Lake City: Bookcraft, 1978), 35.

28. Spencer W. Kimball, "Guidelines to Carry Forth the Work of God in Cleanliness," *Ensign,* May 1974, 7.

29. *Preach My Gospel,* 187–88.

30. Boyd K. Packer, "The Brilliant Morning of Forgiveness," *New Era,* April 2005, 7.

31. Packer, "The Brilliant Morning of Forgiveness," *New Era,* April 2005, 6–7.

32. Marvin J. Ashton, Regional Representatives Seminar, October 4, 1973.

33. Kenneth Cope, "Hear Them Cry," from *Voices* (Embryo Music, 1991).

34. Carol Lynn Pearson, "Secrets," *New Era,* March 1984, 17–18.

35. Susan Evans McCloud, "Lord, I Would Follow Thee," in *Hymns,* no. 220.

36. Gary and Joy Lundberg, *I Don't Have to Make Everything All Better* (New York: Penguin Books, 2000).

37. See Craig A. Cardon, "Moving Closer to Him," *Ensign,* November 2006, 94–96.

38. Gordon B. Hinckley, *Be Thou an Example* (Salt Lake City: Deseret Book, 1981), 137.

39. Vaughn J. Featherstone, *Hold Up Your Light* (Salt Lake City: Bookcraft, 1986), 68–69.

40. Gordon B. Hinckley, *Discourses of President Gordon B. Hinckley, Volume 1: 1995–1999* (Salt Lake City: Deseret Book, 2005), 433.

41. Parley P. Pratt, "Do What Is Right," in *Hymns,* no. 237.

42. See Neal A. Maxwell, "From the Beginning," *Ensign,* November 1993, 20.

43. See Christian Smith, *Soul Searching: The Religious and Spiritual Lives of American Teenagers* (New York: Oxford University Press, 2005).

44. Hinckley, "This Is the Work of the Master," *Ensign,* May 1995, 70.

45. Dr. Seuss, *My Many Colored Days* (New York: Knopf Books for Young Readers, 1996).

46. Joe J. Christensen, "Ten Ideas to Increase Your Spirituality," *Ensign,* March 1999, 58.

47. See Kimball, *Lengthen Your Stride,* 421–22.

48. See "Loving My Wayward Child," *Ensign,* September 2001, 26–28.

49. Robert E. Wells, "Peace on Earth," *Ensign,* September 2001, 31.

50. Mother Teresa, www.quotationspage.com, 33646 from *Classic Quotes* (accessed May 22, 2007).

51. Joseph Fielding McConkie, *Here We Stand* (Salt Lake City: Deseret Book, 1995), 171.

52. David O. McKay, in Conference Report, Apr. 1959, 122.

INDEX

▲ ▲ ▲

ABOUT THE AUTHORS

Brad Wilcox was born and reared in Provo, Utah, apart from childhood years spent in Ethiopia, Africa. He is an associate professor in the Department of Teacher Education at Brigham Young University. He also teaches at Church education programs such as Especially for Youth and Campus Education Week. He enjoys writing for Church magazines and has published many books and talks on CD. His latest works include *Where Do Babies Come From?; The Prophet and the Plates;* and *Red Lights, Green Lights, and Personal Revelation.* As a young man he served a mission in Viña del Mar, Chile, and returned to that country as mission president of the Chile Santiago East Mission from 2003–06. He currently serves as second counselor in the presidency of the BYU 4th Stake and as a member of the Mission Presidents' Advisory Committee. He and his wife, Debi, have four children.

Russell Wilcox grew up in Provo, Utah, where he graduated from Provo High School in 2003. He also lived for a time in New Zealand while his father directed a study-abroad program there. Russell received his associate's degree from Brigham Young University—Idaho and is finishing his bachelor's degree in humanities at Brigham Young University in Provo. He served in the Spain Málaga Mission from 2004–06 and currently serves as president of the elders quorum in his ward. He enjoys teaching at the Missionary

Training Center in Provo and has also spoken at BYU Women's Conference and at Campus Education Week. Russell has written several articles for the *New Era*. He and his wife, Trish, were married just before this book was published.